"Karl Kuhn's book on Luke allows readers to appreciate the author and his work. Kuhn provides a portrait of an elite person well studied in Israel's traditions who is willing and able to venture a meaning of those traditions in light of the radical conviction that Jesus and the earliest followers were continuing to unveil God's news. Luke's literacy, artistry, and even his risk taking are especially enhanced by Kuhn's appreciation for the context of similar authors."

— Kenneth G. Stenstrup, PhD
Assistant Professor of Theology
Saint Mary's University, Minnesota

"It is a pleasure to read such a well-written book that takes the reader into the social world of the author of the Third Gospel. Dr. Kuhn focuses on Luke's literary skills, motifs, and agenda as a way to construct him as a highly literate Jew who once belonged to the social elite but who then turned his back on his status in response to Jesus' critique of the wealthy and his claims as Lord. The book claims that Luke's purpose is to encourage others from among the elite to follow him in this counter-cultural move. Dr. Kuhn has a contemporary North American audience particularly in mind and pitches his book at young scholars and students looking to know something about literacy/illiteracy and wealth and status in the Palestinian world of the first century. In addition, Dr. Kuhn is comfortable in his grasp of current issues in Lukan studies and is a useful and clear guide for the reader in that wider field of scholarship. I recommend this book highly and look forward to more in this significant series on Paul's Social Network."

— Rick Strelan
Associate Professor in New Testament and
Early Christianity
University of Queensland, Brisbane

Paul's Social Network: Brothers and Sisters in Faith
Bruce J. Malina, Series Editor

Luke

The Elite Evangelist

Karl Allen Kuhn

A Michael Glazier Book

LITURGICAL PRESS
Collegeville, Minnesota

www.litpress.org

A Michael Glazier Book published by Liturgical Press

Cover design by Ann Blattner. *Saint Paul,* fresco fragment, Roma, 13th century.

Scripture texts in this work are taken from the New Revised Standard Version Bible © 1989, Division of Christian Education of the National Council of the Churches of Christ in the United States of America. Used by permission. All rights reserved.

1   2   3   4   5   6   7   8   9

Library of Congress Cataloging-in-Publication Data

Kuhn, Karl Allen, 1967–
       Luke : the elite evangelist / Karl Allen Kuhn.
          p.   cm. — (Paul's social network: brothers and sisters in faith)
       "A Michael Glazier Book."
       Includes bibliographical references and index.
       ISBN 978-0-8146-5305-0 — ISBN 978-0-8146-8002-5 (e-book)
       1. Luke, Saint.   2. Paul, the Apostle, Saint—Friends and associates.   I. Title.

    BS2465.K84 2010
    226.4'067—dc22

                                                                2010021433

For my parents, Allen and Barbara

CONTENTS

PREFACE

Human beings are embedded in a set of social relations. A social network is one way of conceiving that set of social relations in terms of a number of persons connected to one another by varying degrees of relatedness. In the early Jesus group documents featuring Paul and coworkers, it takes little effort to envision the apostle's collection of friends and friends of friends that is the Pauline network.

This set of brief books consists of a description of some of the significant persons who constituted the Pauline network. For Christians of the Western tradition, these persons are significant ancestors in faith. While each of them is worth knowing by themselves, it is largely because of their standing within that web of social relations woven about and around Paul that they are of lasting interest. Through this series we hope to come to know those persons in ways befitting their first-century Mediterranean culture.

Bruce J. Malina
Creighton University
Series Editor

ACKNOWLEDGMENTS

Several people have helped me shape this work into the form in which it now appears. My colleagues participating in the Social Scientific Criticism Task Force of the Catholic Biblical Association have taught me much about this form of analysis and its benefits for biblical study. My own investigation of Scripture has been enriched from the many insights they have shared in our conversations during the last several years I have participated in the seminar, and those conversations sowed many seeds that germinated in the study offered here. In addition to the assistance provided by these colleagues, three individuals served as my readers for earlier versions of the manuscript: Fred Kramer, Becky Johnston, and Kathryn Kuhn. To them I owe much appreciation for their generous gift of time, encouragement, careful reading, and insight. Lakeland librarian Joe Pirillo graciously and ably processed numerous interlibrary loan requests for me, making my research of literacy in the Roman Empire much easier from our setting in rural Wisconsin. I am also grateful to Liturgical Press for their commitment to the Paul's Social Network Series, especially Hans Christoffersen, and to Bruce Malina, the series editor.

I also give thanks for the many blessings I receive in my ministry of teaching and learning at Lakeland College. As a college of the United Church of Christ with an undergraduate program in religion and a graduate program in theology, Lakeland has granted me many opportunities to shape my understanding of Scripture and faith in conversation with students, colleagues, and members of the wider church community. Above all, I give thanks for my parents, Allen and Barbara, to whom this volume is dedicated, my wife, Kathryn, and our children, Joshua and Clare, whose support and love in this and many other endeavors are a source of tremendous blessing and joy.

INTRODUCTION

Exploring Luke's Identity

Like the other volumes in the Paul's Social Network Series, this short book aims to explore a certain companion of Paul within the social context of the first-century Mediterranean world. A distinctive feature of this series has been its display of social-scientific methods and models. It has also sought to demonstrate the usefulness of these methods in helping us better understand how companions of Paul may have been shaped by, participated in, and perhaps resisted the dominant social forces of their time. Here I too will make use of social-scientific concepts and models to explore the social location and other features of the companion of Paul who penned the impressive literary and theological achievement we call the Gospel of Luke and Acts of the Apostles (henceforth referred to as "Luke-Acts").[1] In particular, I will draw from current anthropological theories on social stratification in the ancient world and how such stratification governed and legitimated the inequitable distribution of power and resources. This investigation will be interwoven with two additional pursuits: an exploration of literacy in the Greco-Roman world, focusing on Hellenistic and Israelite sources, and a critical analysis (literary, historical, and rhetorical) of the evangelist's writings. Perhaps among the contributions this volume may make to the series is its example of how social-scientific analysis may be profitably employed alongside other forms of critical investigation commonly utilized in New Testament (NT) studies.

Before getting to the focus of the study, I need to offer some justification for my claim that the writer of Luke-Acts was one of Paul's companions. The goal of the present chapter is to provide that justification along with some informed speculation regarding the evangelist's ethnicity. These matters will briefly entangle us in the sometimes tedious realm of scholarly debate. But I will attempt to lead you through this cacophony of voices as efficiently as possible so that we can then move to that dimension of the evangelist which is the focus of this book: his social location.

The Writer of Luke-Acts and Paul

Luke, the Physician

The question of whether the writer of Luke-Acts was a companion of Paul is often connected to the debate regarding the traditional ascription of these writings to "Luke, the physician," who accompanied Paul on at least some of his missionary travels. That there was a "Luke" who was an associate of Paul is indicated in the following epistle texts:

1) In Colossians 4:14, Paul refers to "Luke the beloved physician," whose greetings Paul sends to the church at Colossae along with others.

2) In 2 Timothy 4:11, Paul urges that Timothy come quickly, for "only Luke is with me."

3) In Philemon 24, "Luke" is included among a list of "fellow workers" who send their greetings to Philemon.

We must grant the possibility that more than one "Luke" might be in view in these passages. However, that the epistles each have in mind the same figure is strongly suggested by the fact that they each name a certain Demas in connection with the Luke they reference. Demas is identified by Paul as one who—along with Luke—also sends his greetings (Col 4:14; Philemon 24), or as one who has abandoned Paul and Luke (2 Tim 4:11), suggesting that he was a companion or associate of Luke and Paul. To propose that the epistles identify more than one "Luke" in these passages entails that there must have been more than one Luke of note in the early church connected both to Paul's mission and to another figure named Demas. This is certainly possible, but it seems much more likely that a single Luke is here in view.

More difficult to ascertain is the relationship between the Luke named in the epistles and the writer of Luke-Acts. Later ecclesial tradition assigns the authorship of the gospel and Acts to Luke, the companion of Paul named in the epistles. Five surviving witnesses dating from the end of the second century into the early third century CE provide this testimony.[2] The title, "Gospel according to Luke" is found in the oldest extant (surviving) manuscript of the text, P[75], a papyrus codex dating from 175 to 225 CE. The Muratorian Canon, dated by most to 170 to 190, lists a number of works deemed authoritative by Christians, including most of what later comprise the NT, including "The third book of the Gospel: According to Luke." The canonical list further states, "This Luke was a physician." The second-century theologian Irenaeus also names Luke as a companion of Paul and the writer of Luke-Acts and considers him the same figure identified in Paul's epistles. In addition, the ancient, extratextual "Prologue to the Gospel," also dating from the end of the second century, attributes the gospel's authorship (and that of Acts) to Luke and identifies him as "a Syrian of Antioch, by profession a physician, the disciple of the apostles, and later a follower of Paul until his martyrdom."[3] Finally, Tertullian, in his writings opposing Marcion, similarly identifies the writer of the third gospel as Luke, a companion of Paul, and describes Luke's gospel as a digest of Paul's teaching. These multiple witnesses clearly show that the tradition identifying Luke the physician and companion of Paul as the writer of Luke-Acts was firmly established by the end of the second century.

Many scholars, however, debate the reliability of these traditions due to the fact that the gospels themselves are anonymous and the earliest of these traditions date to about one hundred years after Luke-Acts was composed. Moreover, as I discuss below, some scholars point to several discrepancies between Acts and Paul's letters in their respective portraits of Paul and his teaching as decisive evidence against the claim that the writer of Acts was a companion of Paul.

The Writer of Luke-Acts

I do not intend to lead you any further into the debate over whether the "Luke" mentioned in the epistles is the writer of Luke-Acts. I am inclined to believe the traditional attributions since I don't find the arguments against them all that compelling. But at present, we lack the data we would need to render a more certain verdict. More convincing, it seems to me, is the evidence indicating that the writer of Luke-Acts, whether "Luke, the physician" or not, was a sometime companion of Paul and eyewitness to certain events of his ministry. The evidence supporting this judgment is the occurrence of the first-person plural ("We") to refer to Paul and his comrades in several places throughout Acts. To be more specific, the narrator includes himself among those called to preach the gospel in Macedonia (Acts 16:10) and then travels with Paul and others to Philippi (20:5-6). From there, "we" journeyed to Assos, Mitylene, Samos, and Miletus (20:13-15) and eventually to Tyre, Ptolemais, and Jerusalem (21:1-17). Later, after Paul's hearings, the writer includes himself in the troop that set sail with Paul (now a prisoner) for Italy (27:1), finally arriving in Rome after a shipwreck at sea and a three-month winter layover on the island of Malta (28:11-16). In the view of many modern readers, the implication of this grammatical anomaly, commonly referred to as the "we passages," is that the writer intended his audience to understand that he himself participated in some of the events of Paul's life that he narrates.

This claim is also not without its detractors, as a number of scholars have challenged the view that the writer of Luke-Acts was actually one of Paul's companions for some of his missionary travels. The primary factor motivating their skepticism is, as noted above, the discrepancies one finds between the portrait of Paul presented in Acts and what can be known about Paul from his letters. The more salient of these inconsistencies include the following:

1. In Acts, Paul is portrayed as a great miracle worker, but no mention of this is made in Paul's letters.

2. Acts never portrays Paul as writing letters and gives no indication of having read any of Paul's letters.

3. Paul's letters offer accounts of Paul's movements and experiences that sometimes conflict with or are not corroborated by Acts, such as the number of his visits to Jerusalem after his conversion, his sojourn to Arabia (Gal 1:17-22), Paul's various floggings and shipwrecks (2 Cor 11:24-25), the collection for the Jerusalem church as Paul's motive for his return to Jerusalem (Rom 16:1-4), and his plans to preach in Spain (Rom 15:24, 28).

4. Paul's theology as can be discerned from his letters conflicts with the preaching of Paul as presented in Acts, including subjects such as the use and place of the law, the salvific significance of the resurrection, and the importance of the return of Christ.

In light of these inconsistencies, some scholars have looked for explanations of the "we passages" in Acts apart from the supposition that the writer was intending to present himself as a companion of Paul. Some have claimed that the first-person narration in certain passages simply reflects the writer's use of an eyewitness source for these events. The writer then retained the use of the first person to signal to the reader that his narrative here is based on eyewitness accounts.[4] Offering another explanation, Vernon K. Robbins cites numerous examples to show that there was a "sea voyage" genre in first-century Greco-Roman literature and that this literature often employed first-person narration as a stylistic device.[5] According to Robbins, the occur-rence of the first-person plural in these passages reflects the writer's use of this convention. Robbins also argues that Luke may have been led to utilize this device to convey his sense of solidarity with Paul and the Pauline mission and even to invite his readers to feel as though they are participating in the story themselves.

There are, however, serious problems with each of these two attempts to account for the "we passages" in Acts. Very few scholars have found convincing Robbins' claim that within "sea voyage" literature of antiquity the use of first-person narrative was a common literary device.[6] Ben Witherington, in his com-mentary on Acts, goes so far to say that "it can now be said with a high degree of certainty that there was no *convention* in antiq-uity for sea voyages to be recorded in the first person."[7] With-erington cites studies showing that first-person narration only typically occurred in sea voyage accounts that were part of entire works that narrated in the first person and that there are as many or more sea voyage accounts relayed in the third person. Even more importantly, many have noted that sea voyages are re-corded elsewhere in Acts where the first person is not used (Acts 13:4, 13; 14:26; 17:4; 18:18, 21; 20:1-2) and that the first-person narration in Acts is also employed to recount events that take place on land (e.g., 21:8-18).

The chief problem with Luke's supposed use of an eyewitness source as a means of accounting for the appearance of the first-person narration is that there are no other indications that such a source is being employed. The grammar, syntax, and vocabu-lary of the "we passages" is consistent with the rest of Luke-Acts.[8] One might argue that the writer has thoroughly reworked the source yet still kept its first-person narration, but that would be to argue the writer's use of an eyewitness source on the basis of the first-person narration alone. It also begs the question as to why the writer would retain the first person only in these select instances and not in other sections of Luke-Acts. Why is it only here that the writer of Luke-Acts wants to indicate that he has made use of eyewitness testimony?

There is, in my view, a better way to account for the supposed inconsistencies between Paul's letters and Acts. Joseph Fitzmyer points out, based on our best efforts to reconstruct the chronology of Paul as presented by Acts, that the writer of Luke-Acts was at most an occasional companion of Paul. Moreover,

> [this chronology] would reveal that Luke was not with Paul during the major part of his missionary activity, or during the period when Paul's most important letters were written. It would also mean that Luke was not on the scene when Paul was facing the major crises in his evangelization of the eastern Mediterranean world, e.g., the Judaizing problem, the struggle with the factions in Corinth, or the questions that arose in Thessalonica. Luke would not have been with Paul when he was formulating the essence of his theology or wrestling with the meaning of the gospel. This would explain why there is such a difference between the Paul of Acts and the Paul of Paul's letters.[9]

Fitzmyer admits that the writer of Luke-Acts may have been unfamiliar with Paul's letters, but this only further helps us to account for the differences between Acts and Paul's own description of his travels, and his perspectives on *Torah*, resurrection, and Christ's return, as noted in (4) above.[10]

Still another factor that may account for inconsistencies in some of the historical details between Acts and Paul's letters is simply the amount of time that had passed between Paul's ministry and the writing of the work. Most date Paul's arrival in Rome between 56 and 61 CE, and this is the last indication from the "we passages" that the narrator was with Paul. This potentially means that our writer wrote his work around twenty to thirty years after his time with Paul, presuming a dating for Acts around 80 to 85 CE.

Finally, it is commonly argued that the more salient differences in the theology of Paul between Acts and Paul's own letters may be simply due to the fact that the writer has recast certain features of Paul's teaching in order to have the main heroes of his

narrative more closely mirror his own perspective. This need
not imply, however, that the writer of Luke-Acts was personally
unacquainted with Paul. He may have known Paul very well.
But writing two to three decades later, he felt that certain features
of Paul's ministry needed to be given greater emphasis and
others downplayed. Similarly, Rick Strelan argues:

> I suggest that Luke is not simply a follower of Paul, meekly
> repeating what Paul stood for. It is fairly clear that he does
> not do that. Nor does he misunderstand Paul. He probably
> understood him very well, and from that perspective felt
> that he could—indeed that he must—modify Paul, provide
> a balance, and so protect everything that Paul stood for
> against the wolves that were threatening to rip the flock
> apart (Acts 20). The "wolves" might have been those who
> took Paul's arguments to their logical conclusion. They
> might have been the forerunners of the Marcionites. In a
> sense, they probably held Paul more to be their hero than
> Luke did! Luke thought Paul was in need of some revision,
> some reclaiming from the wolves; and his thought needed
> some balancing and nuancing along more conservative
> lines. In other words, I suggest that Luke is the controller
> of Paul and wants to present a balance, even a counter-
> balance to Paul himself and other interpreters of Paul.[11]

Among the elements of Paul's teaching that Luke may have de-
emphasized is Paul's perspective on the law's provisional and
now transcended nature and his setting aside of much Israelite
legal tradition. In an account intended in part to demonstrate
Christianity's rootedness in Israelite tradition, Luke-Acts
"sketches the character of Paul in Jewish contours with Pharisaic
overtones."[12] For this reason, Paul is presented as agreeing with
the verdict of the Jerusalem Conference that Gentiles follow at
least some of the dietary restrictions (Acts 15), as maintaining a
close connection to James and the Jerusalem church, and as participating in purification rites to demonstrate his allegiance to
Torah (21:17-26).

To summarize, the intermittent nature of his companionship with Paul, the intervening period of twenty to thirty years between that companionship and the writing of Luke-Acts, and the writer's interest in incorporating Paul into his own theological and rhetorical objectives provide plausible explanations—either individually or in some combination—for the differences we find between Luke-Acts and Paul's letters. For this reason, I think it best to understand the function of the "we passages" in the way they are most naturally regarded by readers: to indicate that the writer participated in some of the events he describes. Thus, the companion of Paul on which we will focus in the following pages is the one who traveled with Paul for a time, wrote the impressive work we know as Luke-Acts, and devoted a large segment of his two-volume work to recounting (and recasting) Paul's ministry. For convenience sake, we will henceforth refer to Paul's sometime companion and writer of Luke-Acts as "Luke."

Luke: Son of Israel or Gentile?

Just as the authorship of Luke-Acts has been a contested issue among scholars, so too has the ethnicity of the writer implied by the work.[13] While space limitations do not allow for a thorough review of this debate, we can succinctly summarize its main contours. The two strongest pieces of evidence in favor of Luke being Gentile are church tradition, which considers Luke a "Syrian of Antioch," and the reference to Luke in Colossians 4. In Colossians 4:10-11, Paul names Aristarchus, Mark the cousin of Barnabus, and Jesus who is called Justus, as "the only ones of the circumcision among my co-workers for the kingdom of God." Paul then goes on to list others who also send along their greetings, including Epaphras, "who is one of you," Luke, and Demas. The implication is that Epaphras, Luke, and Demas are not "ones of the circumcision," and thus not children of Israel.

Those arguing that Luke was most likely Israelite point above all else to his intimate knowledge of Israel's Scriptures. This familiarity is exhibited in a number of ways: direct citation and widespread allusion to those Scriptures throughout Luke-Acts, the patterning of characters in Luke-Acts after characters in the Israelite Scriptures, the use of a Semitic or Septuagintal style of Greek in the infancy narrative, and the use of literary devices (such as direct and indirect discourse, widespread allusion to sacred tradition, the tendency to situate the events depicted within the larger story of God's dealings with Israel) that more closely parallel their use in Israelite tradition than in other Greco-Roman writings (see chap. 2).

In addition, Luke shows concern for the maintenance of at least some forms of Torah piety. As noted above, Luke presents Paul as more favorably disposed to Israelite law and practice than is reflected in Paul's letters. Both Jesus and the witnesses of the early church honor the Sabbath by attending synagogue or the temple (Luke 4:16; Acts 2:46; 3:1; 5:20; 13:5; 17:2; 21:26). Also, leading characters of his infancy narrative are presented as epitomes of Torah piety. They serve in the temple (Luke 1:5-23; 2:25-38), circumcise their offspring (1:59; 2:21), and make the offerings required of new parents (2:22-24). Another telling piece of evidence that comes from Luke's gospel is his handling of the tradition found in Mark 7:1-23. In this story, Jesus responds to the Pharisees' criticism of his disciples for not washing their hands before they ate by stating that it is not what goes into a person that renders them unclean but sinful actions and attitudes toward others (7:18-23). While reporting Jesus' response, lest the reader miss the point of the story (as Mark understands it), Mark explains in a parenthetical aside, "Thus he declared all foods clean" (7:19). Matthew follows Mark's account closely but omits the parenthetical comment declaring all foods clean. Luke, however, fails to mention the entire story. Accordingly, in Acts 15 Luke records the verdict of the Jerusalem Conference that Gentile Christians do not need to be circumcised but should participate in some of the dietary restrictions and abstain from certain foods (thus God's command for Peter to "kill and eat" unclean animals in the vision of Acts 10 is likely meant to be taken as a metaphor, not literally). While there are plenty of elements of Luke's narrative that challenge traditional Israelite notions of purity and piety, especially with respect to "unclean" and marginalized persons, it seems important to Luke that some dimensions of Torah practice be maintained.

Still another piece of evidence suggesting that Luke is Israelite, and evidence rarely considered in the debate, are several close parallels between Luke's gospel and writings found among the Dead Sea Scrolls. These parallels suggest that Luke was familiar with and had access to some of the texts collected by the Qumran community. These parallels consist of the "Son of God" text (4Q246; cf. Luke 1:32-35), the "Pierced Messiah" text (4Q285; cf. Luke 4:16-21), the "Resurrection Text" (4Q521; cf. Luke 4:18), and the "Song of Miriam" (4Q365, frag. 6; Luke 1:46-55). Speaking of these parallels, George Brooke states that they suggest "the place of Luke in preserving, in its special material and in its writer's handling of inherited traditions, the viewpoint of a strand of Judaism which can be found in some fragmentary scroll texts."[14]

In my view, the weight of the evidence falls in favor of Luke being of the House of Israel. While not impossible that a Gentile could immerse himself in Israelite sacred tradition to the extent that Luke clearly did, I think such intimate knowledge of that tradition in Luke's day is far more likely of an Israelite person than a Gentile. Even if Luke were a Gentile convert to Israel's tradition, one wonders if he would have had the access to written texts and instruction he would have needed to gain such a familiarity with Israelite sacred tradition. There is also the curious matter of Luke's familiarity with texts that were also housed at Qumran. While copies of those texts could have existed outside of the Qumran community, I think it far more likely that Luke would have come across such writings, let alone even known about their existence, if he were a son of Israel and had Essene acquaintances than if he were a Gentile.

How then are we to account for the evidence suggesting that Luke was Gentile? Luke's identification as a "Syrian from

Antioch" in the earliest strata of church testimony (first to second century) comes from a single source, the extratextual Prologue to the Gospel, a hundred years after the writing of the gospel. Moreover, Luke's identity as a "Syrian" does not necessarily entail that he is not Israelite, both religiously and ethnically. The term could be meant as a geographic (indicating Syrian Antioch rather than Pisidian Antioch) rather than an ethnic marker. Due to the exiles of the eighth and sixth centuries BCE, Israelites could be found throughout the entire Mediterranean region in Luke's day. Or, Luke could be from a family of mixed ethnicity that has thoroughly embraced its Israelite heritage. More problematic is the passage from Colossians 4, in which "Luke the physician" is not included among those who are "men of the circumcision." Strelan argues, however, that the phrase need not be taken as referring to Israelites who were part of the Pauline mission as opposed to Paul's Gentile associates. Instead, what the phrase likely has in view is not differences in *ethnicity* but in *practice*. Thus, "those men 'of the circumcision' probably refers to those Israelite followers of Christ who were ritually strict compared to the ritually lax Paul; it does not infer that those not 'of the circumcision' were not of Israel."[15]

Even More Important—Luke's Social Location

I generally regard as sage advice the oft-repeated claim that the particular identity of the evangelists is of little consequence for understanding their writings. It is what they wrote about Jesus and the kingdom of God that matters, and knowing this or that about features of their personhood would change little, if anything at all, about our understanding of their work. Does it really matter if the writer of Luke-Acts was a physician, or a companion of Paul, or Israelite, or just a really gifted Gentile historian who gained access to a lot of good sources? Would it really help us better understand what he said and the reason he said it? Perhaps it is simply better for us to work with what we have before us, the text itself, and our general knowledge of the first-century Mediterranean world than to chase after the ghostly contours of Luke's identity.

Perhaps. But "Bible-geeks" (like me) will still speculate on such things, as trivial as they might seem. And yet, there may very well be a feature of Luke's identity that is relatively accessible to us. It might also be one that can sharpen our understanding of the third evangelist and his two volumes on Christian origins he painstakingly composed, even though it is given little attention in Lukan scholarship. That feature is Luke's *social location*. As I use the term, "social location" refers to where Luke stood—socially and economically—relative to others in his society. But investigating Luke's social location entails more than just determining Luke's place on the social scale. It also includes determining Luke's proximity to those in power and the extent to which Luke shares in that power. It involves Luke's access to resources (food, shelter, health, leisure time) and the culturally shared perspectives that would have legitimated Luke's access to those resources based on his social location. It is the aim of this work to shed some light on this little-explored dimension of Luke's identity and to offer some brief reflection on how it helps us to understand more fully the rhetorical edge of his writing. We will begin in chapter 1 by investigating what will serve as the primary index for assessing Luke's social location: the relationship between social location and literacy in the Greco-Roman world, including Roman Palestine. Chapter 2 will examine Luke's level of literacy, focusing on his familiarity with grammar, rhetoric, and other literary devices to determine his probable social status. Chapter 3 will describe Luke's life and the world he knew as a member of the social elite and how knowing this helps us better appreciate the countercultural contours of his testimony. Finally, the conclusion will build upon the findings of the study, offering a brief "portrait of Luke" that draws together the strands of Luke's companionship with Paul, his Israelite identity, his social location, and his radical witness to the gospel of Jesus Messiah.

CHAPTER 1

Literacy in Luke's World

For the vast majority of human societies today, the written word is a basic element of the social fabric. Written communication, whether print or digital, is a pervasive and essential mode of dialogue in nearly every aspect of daily living. Indeed, oral communication and face-to-face conversation still occur quite frequently (thank goodness!). But think for a moment how much of your social interaction is in the form of written language. How many e-mails, text messages, blogs, Facebook, Twitter posts, or handwritten notes did you compose today? How many of them did you read? How many web sites, articles, books, recipes, road signs, graffiti, television graphics, product instructions, advertisements did you study, peruse, or at least offer a passing glance? Written communication is ubiquitous in our culture and in most cultures around the globe. It would be next to impossible to go a day without participating in it.

The ability to understand and create written exchange—*literacy*—is also widespread in today's world. According to UNESCO, literacy rates among persons age fifteen and above in most developed nations are above 99 percent. While literacy skills undoubtedly vary considerably among the citizens of these countries, that nearly the entirety of these populations has at least a basic proficiency in reading and writing is an astounding figure, especially when viewed against the backdrop of the last several millennium of human history. For many of us, of course, literacy is something we simply take for granted—a skill or ability as basic as walking and talking. For the vast majority of the time chronicled by humans, however, very few people could read, and cultures were far less dependent on the written word.

As we prepare ourselves to explore literacy within Luke's world, it is thus good for us to be aware that we are entering a world that is in many respects, including in the use of written communication, quite different than our own. At the same time, we should be forewarned that the subject of literacy in the Greco-Roman world (the world shaped by the empires of Greece and Rome from roughly fourth century BCE to the fifth century CE) is not as simple as figuring out how many people could read and write. We will be interested in finding out what researchers say about those figures. But viewed through a social-scientific lens and with an eye toward the matter at hand (assessing Luke's social location), there are several other dimensions of literacy we will want to explore. For instance, what were the various levels of literacy? What were the relationships between literacy, education, economics, and social standing? What role did the written word play in social control, maintenance of the status quo, or in social change? How did written language impact religious communities and their doctrinal development or preservation? We will investigate these dimensions of literacy as we engage the topic in five broad strokes.

Five Dimensions of Literacy in Luke's World

1) *In Luke's Day, Literacy Was Restricted to a Small Minority of the Population*

Until relatively recently, it was not uncommon for scholars to propose that literacy rates in the Greek and Roman Empires were relatively high, at times including the majority of their populations. With the advent of William V. Harris' landmark study, *Ancient Literacy*, however, that optimism among historians studying the topic has eroded dramatically.[1] Harris argued, based on investigations of increased literacy rates in early-modern and modern Europe, that "writing ceases to be the arcane accomplishment of a small professional or social or religious elite only when certain preconditions are fulfilled and *only* when strong positive forces are present to bring the change about."[2] The chief precondition for mass literacy that Harris identified is a *subsidized educational system*. Such a mechanism is needed to allow for widespread access to literacy training across a broad spectrum of the populace, including the peasant majority.[3] Harris argues that ancient Greece and Rome never saw, in any sustained sense, the necessary political, economic, social, and ideological forces needed to sustain or even create such an educational system. Other preconditions Harris identifies include sufficient population densities (i.e., the majority need to be gathered in cities rather than spread out in rural areas), access to written texts and writing supplies, and an economic system that allowed for and encouraged time for literacy instruction. Harris concludes that, in general, each of these preconditions were also lacking throughout the Greek and Roman Empires.

> The classical world, even at its most advanced, was so lacking in the characteristics which produce extensive literacy that we must suppose that the majority of the people were always illiterate. In most places most of the time, there was no incentive for those who controlled the allocation of resources to aim for mass literacy. Hence the institutional lacunae which would have impeded any movement towards mass literacy—above all the shortage of subsidized schools—were confronted to no more than a slight extent.[4]

Beyond identifying features essential to creating widespread literacy and noting their lack in the Greco-Roman world, much of Harris' volume takes up a wide-ranging survey of epigraphic and literary material to support his thesis and to provide data for estimating literacy rates in antiquity. The evidence he details indicates that among certain social groups, and in certain segments of economic and political life, written communication played a very important role (more on this later). On the whole, however, the available evidence confirms his assessment that the ability to read and write, beyond the rudimentary functions of signing one's name, recognize the shape of some common words, or roughly scratch out a receipt (often called, "semiliteracy") was limited to a select few. Harris finds that in the Roman Empire of the first century BCE, it is "unlikely that the overall literacy of the western providences even rose into the range of 5-10%,"[5] and the literacy rates of the empire as a whole were no greater than 10 percent.[6] For Egypt and other eastern provinces such as Judea, Harris suggests that rates of literacy may have been higher than was common in the West but were still confined to a small proportion of the population.[7] Moving into the first century of the Common Era, Harris concludes that "the great increase in epigraphical production in Rome and Italy from the time of Augustus onward, perhaps even more from the first century A.D., makes it likely that at least a slightly higher proportion of the population was able to read and write." He immediately cautions, however, that "this is as far as the hypotheses may legitimately go."[8]

Harris' conclusions on the limited extent of literacy in the ancient world have been largely adopted by subsequent treatments of the topic. While some have challenged Harris' handling of the evidence at certain points and have sought to nuance his findings or argue for a somewhat higher rate of literacy, his basic claim that the ability to read and write in the Hellenistic and Roman world never extended beyond a minority of adult males and a tiny minority of adult females has become the standard view.[9]

Scholars examining Israelite literacy in Palestine have reached similar conclusions. After a survey of the use of Scripture, commentary, and scribal practices in Palestine, H. Gregory Snyder concludes, "In Palestine, most people did not, indeed, could not, read and interpret the texts that governed the details of their religious, economic and private life. That task fell to the scribes and teachers of the law."[10] Especially telling on this point is evidence that comes from the Dead Sea Scrolls. We might be led to expect a higher rate of literacy among the Qumran community given its interest in and production of sacred texts. Synder points out, however, that "scribal errors in the Habakkuk commentary show that the writer was copying on a letter by letter basis, perhaps not fully comprehending what he was writing."[11] This is remarkable in light of the central importance the community placed on scriptural interpretation, even to the point of imposing severe injunctions on those who misread—accidental or not—the Torah.[12] Despite such reverence for the traditions in their keeping, "it is not unlikely that the literacy among some copyists in the Qumran community was marginal."[13]

Martin Jaffee points out that, on the one hand, Palestinian society of the last centuries of the Second Temple period (spanning from 515 BCE to 70 CE) was, like others in the Greco-Roman world, "intimately familiar with the written word."

> Writing—in Greek as well as the native Hebrew and Aramaic—was employed in a variety of economic functions and legal instruments across various social strata. In market and town squares, legends on coins and seals proclaimed the propaganda on behalf of regional minting cities and contenders for political hegemony. Complex works of literature—historical, legal, ethical, hymnodic, and even novelistic—were composed and circulated. Social movements of various kinds embraced ancient, revered books as symbols of identity and authenticity and used the written word polemically to position themselves in relation to each other along a spectrum of social and religious questions. There was even enough of a literary public in the country's three languages to sustain efforts to render important Hebrew texts into Greek and Aramaic.[14]

Written communication, in other words, played an important role in the literary, religious, and legal dimensions of first-century Palestine society. The ability to compose or personally access written communication, however, was limited to a select few. As Jaffee explains:

> But for all its literacy, this was not a bookish society of the type that has existed in the modern world since the development of mass-produced, printed literature. For one thing, the group of people who could actually compose, transcribe, and communicate the contexts of written compositions—whether brief letters or lengthy literary works—was quite small in relation to the society as a whole. Such skills were regarded as esoteric professional acquisitions rather than a general cultural patrimony. Persons possessing them were, for the most part, members of elite scribal guilds associated with official institutions of palace, law court, and temple. Outside such groups, the ability to write was routinely limited to elementary forms of record-keeping.[15]

Catherine Hezser has devoted still another lengthy investigation of literacy among Israelites in Roman Palestine, extending into the seventh century, yet focusing on the rabbinic period after the destruction of the temple. She too concludes, based on the rural character of Palestine, its "pyramidal" educational system that focused its energies on the few best and brightest students, and the lack of surviving epigraphical evidence to the contrary, that Israelite literacy rates in Palestine during this time were very low, even lower than the 10 percent literacy rate Harris estimated for Roman society in general.[16]

2) *In Ancient Greece and Rome, Higher Levels of Literacy and Literary Acumen Were Achieved by Only a Very Select Few*

Following Harris' study, another important exploration of the topic of literacy in ancient Greece and Rome was offered by Teresa Morgan in *Literate Education in the Hellenistic and Roman Worlds*. Morgan's work examines surviving papyri "school texts" from Hellenistic Egypt, in conversation with discussions of education by Greek and Roman writers, to establish what subjects were being taught, to whom they were being taught, and for what purpose.[17] While Morgan's study isn't chiefly concerned with rates of basic literacy, she concurs with Harris' low estimation and additionally argues that only a very small minority went beyond a rudimentary literary education.[18]

The arid climate of Egypt determines, in part, Morgan's focus on Egyptian school texts, since the papyri and wooden tablets used in educational settings survived at a much higher rate in dry sand than in the ancient trash heaps of moister regions of the Greco-Roman world. While geographically limited to Egypt, these hundreds of extant (surviving) scratches, notes, and lessons of Egyptian schoolchildren provide us with a wealth of material for assessing the educational practices within the Greek and Roman Empires. While there were probably regional variations in pedagogy throughout the Mediterranean world, it is likely that the educational practices we can glean from these Egyptian papyri provide us with a representative picture of Greco-Roman educational patterns and strategies. Egypt, like the rest of the Mediterranean region, was thoroughly Hellenized from the third century BCE onward. As Egypt shared in other Hellenistic cultural patterns, so did its people also likely adopt the educational practices common throughout the rest of the Hellenized world.

The value of the papyri is that their combined witness provides us with an account of what literate education was actually like in the centuries leading up to and including the writing of Luke's gospel. Morgan supplements their witness with another valuable set of resources: the writings of Greek and Roman writers on education. While there are some variations in the accounts provided or in the educational practices prescribed by these writers, each of their surviving discussions of *enkyklios paideia*, the "common" or "basic education," are regarded by Morgan as "variations on a theme whose dominant and most remarkable characteristic is still its high degree of uniformity across the Hellenistic and Roman worlds."[19] The following literary subjects are consistently included in the versions of *enkyklios paideia* provided by writers such as Polybius (second century BCE, Greece/Rome), Cicero (first century BCE, Rome), Dionysius of Halicarnassus (first century BCE, Rome), Philo (first cenutry BCE to first century CE, Alexandria), and Quintilian (first century CE, Rome):

1. reading

2. writing

3. grammar (declensions, conjugations, parts of speech)

4. literature (brief commentary on literature and the study of literary forms)

5. rhetoric (literary convention, theory of argumentation, exercises on rhetorical forms and techniques)

6. dialectic (philosophy)[20]

Based on her examination of both the "educationalists" and the school text papyri, Morgan provides the following modification of the *enkyklios paideia* as it was likely practiced in the Hellenistic and Roman eras:

> The elements of which *enkyklios paideia* consists, according to the combined evidence of the papyri and writings of educationalists, are as follows: reading and writing the alphabet; reading and writing lists of syllables and complete words; reading and writing short, then longer extracts of literature; grammar, paraphrase and rhetorical exercises; sometimes rhetoric and occasionally philosophy.[21]

In light of the common elements and diversity found in the papyri, Morgan also concludes that much of the Greco-Roman world followed a "core and periphery" model of education.[22] She cautions that this model shouldn't be viewed as a detailed curriculum: "it is clear from the very earliest exercises that while a wide range of texts and exercises were in use overall, very few of them were *widely* used."[23] At the same time, Morgan finds that there was a "core" of sorts to the educational practices of ancient Egypt.

> The "core" I propose is a core in three senses. It includes what most people learned, what they learned first and, in the case of reading, what they went on practicing the longest. It would include methods of learning to read and write, the reading (and copying and, if we follow the literary sources, memorizing) of gnomic sayings [aphorisms] and the reading of Homer (and Virgil in the Latin-speaking West), since these are the only texts which survive in sufficient numbers and in a sufficiently wide range of hands.[24]

For our purposes, it is instructive to note that two literary elements of the *enkyklios paideia* identified by those writing about education—grammar and rhetoric—are far less frequently attested in the school texts. While belonging to the "core" in the theoretical discussions of education provided by Philo, Quintilian, Cicero, and others, "grammar and rhetoric are peripheral in that few people appear to have learned them and they are virtually all in the most accomplished schoolhands we possess."[25] With these subjects in particular, Morgan finds that those writing on education were defining an ideal that did not reflect the actual educational practices on the ground. Very few, in fact, progressed to the point that they were learning anything more than rudimentary elements of grammar and rhetorical theory. As Morgan summarizes:

> From this it is possible to build up a picture of widespread teaching of the elements of literacy and reading of literature. The next stages of education—grammar and rhetoric—went on in far fewer places. We cannot assume that people who learned to read and write in small towns regularly moved on to larger ones at a later stage of education, though some undoubtedly did so. Not enough grammatical or rhetorical texts survive, even from large centres with papyrus finds of all kinds, for that. It looks rather as though the number of people in Upper Egypt whose education progressed as far as learning grammar and rhetoric was a very small proportion of those who acquired some basic literacy and read some literature.[26]

Morgan's insights help to fill out our picture of literacy in the first-century world. Only a relatively small number of the population could read and/or write. Among those with a basic level of literacy, still a far smaller number progressed to the point of being able to write fluently (grammar) and construct texts employing common literary patterns and strategies of argumentation (rhetoric). Hezser finds the same to be typical of Roman Palestine:

> As already argued in connection with education and schools above, both in ancient Israeliteish and Graeco-Roman society the number of those students who advanced to the higher educational realms will have been very small. The number of those who actually underwent years of rabbinic, rhetorical, or philosophical training and were subsequently accepted by their teachers as rabbis, orators, and philosophers in their own right will have been tiny indeed.[27]

3) *In Luke's World, Literacy, and Especially Advanced Levels of Literacy, Was Primarily Restricted to the Social Elite*

Coinciding with the view of most researchers that literacy was relatively uncommon among the citizens of the Greco-Roman world is the attending claim that the ability to read and write was much more frequently held by members of the upper class than by peasants, artisans, and slaves. Indeed, archaeological evidence tells us that some nonelites and artisans gained a level of what might be called "semiliteracy" or "craftsman literacy." Slaves served as bookkeepers, as did military clerks. Some artisans were able to scratch out a receipt or notes for recordkeeping. Religious devotees among the "common folk" learned to copy and even read their sacred texts. In addition, a few slaves were likely trained as scribes, and many educators were under the employ of wealthy clients.[28] So, the picture of literacy we are to adopt is not that the literate were confined to the social elite. There were exceptions. At the same time, several factors strongly suggest that literacy, especially higher levels of literacy that would have included some proficiency in grammar and rhetoric, was largely restricted to those of the upper class.

ACCESS

One commonly cited factor concentrating literacy among the social elite is simply the severely limited opportunity for educational instruction. As noted by Harris, there was no subsidized, systematic, and widespread system of schools in antiquity. On occasion, resources of the state or of wealthy patrons were designated for schools or for schoolteachers. But this was the exception rather than the rule. According to Harris, buildings from antiquity that can be confidently identified as schools are rare to nonexistent (depending on one's reading of the archaeological evidence), suggesting that schools were likely housed in makeshift structures or at the edge of a forum or portico.[29] Moreover, Harris adds that very few Roman texts suggest the existence of schools large enough to require the presence of several masters at once.[30] If this is accurate, then only a small minority of children living in cities were making use of these schools. Additionally, there is no evidence to suggest that the remaining majority of children, living in small villages and rural areas, would have received even rudimentary training in literacy.

Another point relevant to the matter of access is that Greek and Roman writers frequently expressed contempt for those who taught reading and writing. On the face of it, this may seem rather odd, since these writers and educators certainly shared a high regard for literacy and its benefits. Harris, however, points out that it is scarcely surprising that "the well-to-do belittled those who, while more or less sharing the culture of the elite, sold their knowledge for pathetic sums of money."[31] Harris goes on to add, "We may conclude that the occupation was avoided by almost all educated people who could afford to do so, and the implication of Quintilian that some men became teachers who had themselves not progressed beyond the *primae litterae* is likely to be accurate."[32] If this situation were common, then even if some urban children from the nonelite attended a school with some regularity, most of them could only hope to achieve no more than a basic level of literacy. This may also explain why the elite commonly made use of private tutors for their children rather than relying on schoolteachers. Later in Roman antiquity, Quintilian among others urged the benefits of schooling instead of private tutors. Yet there is telling evidence indicating that as such schools became more attractive to the elite the children of the elite came to dominate them. The school exercises printed in *Corpus Glossariorum Latinorum,* a third-century collection, assume that the boy who attends school comes from a family with several slaves.[33]

Lack of Necessity, Social Obstacles, and Cost

We live in a society in which it is highly advantageous to achieve an advanced (at least in comparison to ancient standards) level of literacy. Those with only rudimentary literacy skills, or none at all, miss out on numerous opportunities in terms of career, economic benefits, social interaction, and social status. To some degree, this was also true in the ancient world. If you were literate, chances were that you had a number of opportunities available to you than would otherwise be the case. The vast majority of occupations performed in the ancient Greco-Roman world, however, and the overwhelming majority of social interaction and transmission of information, did not require even a basic level of literacy. If you were a peasant or artisan, and 97–99 percent of your fellow peasants and artisans could not read or write, and little to nothing of your daily routine required literacy to perform it, why go through several long years of training to acquire it? Why put your children through the burden?[34]

One reason we might offer would be social and economic advancement. As just noted, in our society is it exceedingly common for a high school and college education to be viewed as a prerequisite for economic and social success. There are also greater numbers of older adults returning to educational institutions for degrees and training than ever before in hopes of advancing their careers, improving their economic lot, or simply for personal growth. Shouldn't we just assume that folks in the ancient Mediterranean world similarly embraced the benefits of a literate education? Why wouldn't scores of parents be knocking down the doors of the local school and demanding a seat for their children? Why wouldn't they be lobbying their local officials for more schools and teachers for their villages?

Here is a good example of how we might view the ancient world through the lens of our own time and social experience and thus misconstrue the mindset of most ancient folk and the opportunities available to them. The ancient Mediterranean, like most societies throughout human history, was highly stratified, both economically and socially. Estimates vary slightly among social historians, but most agree that the social elite of the ancient Mediterranean comprised about 2–5 percent of the population. These elite were made up primarily of the governing class but could also include wealthy merchants and prominent "retainers" (those whose job it was to maintain the status quo for the benefit of the elite), such as high-ranking military and government officials and even tax collectors. The vast majority of the population included peasants (free and slave), artisans, unclean or degraded folk (the diseased and mentally ill), and "expendables"—primarily women and children unconnected to a kinship group. While the lot of these lower classes undoubtedly varied among subgroups and could be better or worse depending on the latest harvest, on the whole most of them lived slightly above, at, or below the subsistence level. Moreover, the peasantry was perpetually burdened by heavy taxation and debt, and during the Roman period in Palestine many lost their land and were forced into slavery or tenant farming.

These economic conditions undoubtedly prevented many peasants and artisans from pursuing a literate education. With the vast majority near or below the subsistence level, sending able-bodied children into a village or city with any great regularity to learn their letters (rather than having them help with the fieldwork or home business), and providing them with the relatively expensive materials for writing, was a burden that undoubtedly many could not afford. This is not to say that it did not happen on occasion. But it wouldn't have been common. For most peasant children, a literate education was simply beyond their means.

In addition, a very good case can be made that a social dynamic common in highly stratified societies that severely curtailed the social advancement of individuals was also operative in the ancient Mediterranean. This phenomenon is known to social scientists as "limited good."[35] Anthropologist George Foster offered an explanation of this mindset among the peasantry that has become a standard for many:

> By "Image of Limited Good" I mean that broad areas of peasant behavior are patterned in such a fashion as to suggest that peasants view their social, economic, and natural universes—their total environment—as one in which all of the desired things in life such as land, wealth, health, friendship and love, manliness and honor, respect and status, power and influence, security and safety, exist in finite quantity and are always in short supply, as far as the peasant in concerned. Not only do these and all other "good things" exist in finite and limited quantities, but in addition there is no way directly within peasant power to increase available quantities.[36]

In other words, it was common for peasants to view their situation as part of the social and economic "status quo." They and most among the low-ranking majority typically saw little chance of changing their lot in life, at least in any significant fashion. Modern, Western ideals such as "getting ahead," "making a name for yourself," "following your dreams," and "you can achieve anything if you try hard enough" just were not part of the mindset of the vast majority of peasants and artisans. Scarcity and acceptance of the status quo led to two prominent dimensions of the peasant personality. On the one hand, there was competition among members of the peasantry for the basic necessities among other things. On the other, envy and social reprisal were directed at those who sought to gain a measure of prosperity or status beyond their peers. As Foster argues, "any advantage achieved by one individual or family is seen as a loss to others, and the person who makes what the Western world lauds as 'progress' is viewed as a threat to the stability of the entire community."[37] Similarly, Jerome H. Neyrey and Richard L. Rohrbaugh add:

> For peasants, ancient as well as modern, the world exists as a zero-sum game in which land provides the basic analogy for understanding the world. There is only so much arable land in the world, and it is already all distributed. If one person gets more, someone else has to get less. Moreover, the same is true for all other good things in the world, including water, food, and wealth, as well as respect and fame. . . . The key here is that everything good is already distributed and cannot be increased. . . . Social relations become heavily dependent not just on maintaining what one has in life but also on avoiding the perception of gaining more. To gain is to steal from others. Thus peasants will not tolerate neighbors who acquire beyond what they have.[38]

It may be difficult for us Western folk to wrap our heads around this mindset. And to be sure, there were likely other forces in the ancient world that at least in part worked against the envy and fear that accompanied perceptions of limited good, such as the equally well-established regard for hospitality and the value some placed on generosity. But Neyrey and Rohrbaugh, through the examples they display from biblical and nonbiblical sources, offer a convincing case that the perception of limited good common to highly stratified societies in other times and places was also well established in the ancient Mediterranean world.[39] In conjunction with the economic (and geographic) obstacles noted above that made literate education uncommon among the lower class, the perception of limited good and fear of reprisal would have deterred many peasants and artisans from striving beyond their social and economic means by pursuing a literate education. In short (while keeping in mind the exceptions noted above), there was neither the means nor the motivation to become literate among the heavy majority of the lower classes. Just too many economic and social factors made such a pursuit either irrelevant or too costly.

4) *In Luke's World, Higher Levels of Literacy Were a Valuable Commodity for Those Seeking Honor and Increased Social Status*

The perception of limited good, and the competitive envy that attended it, was not restricted to the peasantry or to the pursuit of physical needs. It was also common among the elite, but it led to a very different kind of social positioning. Instead of functioning as a mechanism curtailing competition and social mobility, the idea of limited good was the driving force behind the "honor game" played by the elite and those wishing to join their ranks. Many, even most, of the interactions between persons in the ancient Mediterranean revolved around the pursuit of honor and challenges to the honor held by others. Honor is commonly identified as one of the most important values in the Greco-Roman world.[40] Put simply and helpfully by Bruce Malina:

> Honor is the value of a person in his or her own eyes (that is, one's claim to worth) *plus* that person's value in the eyes of his or her social group. Honor is a claim to worth along with the social acknowledgement of worth.[41]

Honor could be either *ascribed* or *acquired*. "Ascribed honor" is honor claimed by and granted to a person due to his or her kinship group or authority within and perhaps outside of that kinship group. For instance, if you were born into a prestigious and powerful family, you would likely be granted honor due to your membership in that family. Or, let's say all of the pieces of your early life fell fortuitously in place and you found yourself a member of the emperor's court at a young age. You would also be ascribed honor due to your membership in that elite group.

Let's imagine again that your astute service caught the emperor's eye, and you were appointed as one of the emperor's trusted advisors. Here again you would gain honor not only by your gifted service but also by virtue of your association to another. The emperor's public recognition of you as a chief advisor would ascribe you honor in the eyes of the rest of the court and his loyal subjects (even if they were very jealous of you).

"Acquired honor" is honor that you gain by excelling over others. In other words, this is honor granted to you not simply because of your associations, but by demonstrating your mastery in certain areas. How could such mastery be displayed? Undoubtedly, there were many activities that could potentially enhance a person's reputation: acts of heroism, the donation of funds to a public project, a distinguished military career or other service (as in the example above), eloquent oration, control of one's children, among others. Beyond these avenues to acquired honor, a common form of social exchange often termed *challenge and response* also played a pivotal role in the gain and loss of honor. Challenge and response "is sort of a constant social tug of war, a game of social push and shove."[42] It typically contained the following elements and structure:

> Challenge-response within the context of honor is a sort of interaction in at least three phases: (1) the challenge in terms of some action (word, deed, or both) on the part of the challenger; (2) the perception of the message by both the individual to whom it is directed and the public at large; and (3) the reaction of the receiving individual and the evaluation of the reaction on the part of the public.[43]

To readers of the canonical gospels, this form of social exchange will likely strike them as familiar. Indeed, most of Jesus' interactions with the Pharisees, scribes, and others (sometimes even the disciples) correspond to the challenge and response sequence. At stake in these conflicted gospel scenes is not only how to best understand and follow God's *Torah* but also who is to be judged as one with greater honor. As the gospels tell the story, Jesus repeatedly outdoes his detractors by demonstrating his superior insight into the ways of God: the (1) *challenge* of his opponents is (2) *perceived* by Jesus and the onlookers and met with (3) Jesus' *response*, which is then often celebrated by onlookers as revealing a keener, sometimes astounding, perception of God's will. Having "lost face," Jesus' detractors are silenced and slink away offstage until the time of their next challenge.

Malina and others assume that this form of social exchange was exceedingly common, that it characterized, in fact, nearly all of one's interaction with those outside of one's kinship group.[44] I suspect much social interaction occurred that wasn't so conflicted, but the gospels' own witness to Mediterranean culture reveals that challenge-response was indeed a frequent form of interaction and strongly suggests that the concept of limited good commonly applied to honor as well. People were hungry for honor, and they often sought to outdo one another in obtaining it or to limit the amount of honor held by a perceived rival. Now here is an important point of clarification. To some extent, such social jockeying occurred among individuals throughout the social hierarchy of the Greco-Roman world. "Competition was endemic to ancient society."[45] Peasants were concerned with honor as well. But honor for the peasantry included living into, and not striving beyond, one's social position. Recall Neyrey and Rohrbaugh's comment above: "thus peasants will not tolerate neighbors who acquire beyond what they have."[46] In contrast, the pursuit of honor among the elite was a key vehicle for social advancement.

Teresa Morgan argues that one avenue the social elite pursued in the Roman period for acquiring honor was to obtain and demonstrate higher levels of literary acumen. This was achieved by further study in grammar and literature and, for fewer still, rhetoric.

> At a time when more people were learning to read and write [during the Roman period], those who in an earlier generation would have secured a degree of cultural status simply by being literate, can be imagined to have wanted

to maintain their status in the face of new competition. Grammar may therefore have entered education as an extra rung on the ladder of literate status: something which not everyone would get as far as studying but which did not commit the learner to a further expensive education in rhetoric. Those who learned grammar, but did not go on to study rhetoric, may have formed something of a new, intermediate status-group in literate education.[47]

Citing the evidence of the school texts papyri, Morgan goes on to add:

> The elite sources take for granted that readers have the resources to pick and choose what they learn. The papyri give us a glimpse of a more pressured world, where educational and, no doubt, financial resources were limited, and where having read a few scholia to one's Homer, or having memorized a grammatical table or two, might be a precious measure of cultural status, and having practised even the most elementary rhetorical exercises a rare commodity, a valuable and enviable distinction. The signs of distinction went on being treasured even as Roman culture and power retreated in the Byzantine period.[48]

Keith Hopkins provides a similar account of how literacy played an essential role in defining social status and the pursuit of acquired honor:

> Literary culture was differentiating, in that it provided a single set of criteria by which people's performances, and therefore their membership in different social strata, could be judged. The diversity of educational attainment ranged from the sophisticated to the superficial, from the economically functional to the marginal sub-literate, and to the literate. This diversity of judgement and attainment was important, because it symptomised the permeability of Roman stratification, and underlined the possibility of using education as an effective ladder of social mobility.[49]

In the competitive, agonistic world of the ancient Mediterranean, education and the display of one's knowledge and skill achieved by education served as a common resource for the acquisition of honor among the elite. Increasingly, as Morgan argues, members of the elite turned to learning grammar and rhetoric as a means of setting themselves above their peers. Indeed, as Hopkins cautions, modern academics "have to be wary of exaggerating the importance of bookish knowledge."[50] Of course, that's how we eggheads who write and read books and offer our bookish brilliance to impressionable (in varying degrees) young minds see the world! Nevertheless, even those many years ago in ancient Rome, "it mattered to a surprising degree how you showed, and how much you showed, that you knew something of what was written in books."[51]

5) *In Ancient Rome, Literacy Was Used a Mechanism for Enculturation, Social Stratification, and Control*

I would like to return for a moment to Morgan's observation that literacy skills in the Greco-Roman world were distributed through a "core and periphery" model of education. To summarize, Morgan argues that the Egyptian school text papyri reveal that there was a core of skills, a select group of writers, and types of materials that students commonly engaged. More peripheral were the additional, highly variable writers that were read and the advanced subjects of grammar and rhetoric that increasingly fewer students explored. Morgan proposes that this core and peripheral model served two important social functions. On the one hand, it played an essential role in gathering diverse peoples into Greco-Roman culture. Through the acquisition of literacy, and familiarity with a select group of writers (e.g., Homer and Euripides) and collections of proverbial (gnomic) sayings, diverse peoples from across the Greco-Roman world, especially during the Roman era, became acculturated into Hellenistic literary culture. Through this they gained a sense of identity and belonging and in differing degrees an affiliation with that element of society that controlled access to honor and authority.

This brings us to the second social function of literate education. While literacy and familiarity with revered writers provided a diverse matrix of folk with a sense of participation in the dominant culture, it also served to differentiate between social groups and restrict access to the elite.[52] To put it another way, literate education provided learners with a point of entry into Greco-Roman culture—its values and beliefs, but also its prejudices, hierarchies, competitive environment, and standards of judgment (as also noted by Hopkins above). As described by Morgan:

> "Core and periphery" education performed two social tasks very efficiently. It constituted a mechanism for the admission of cultured non-Greeks or non-Romans into Greek or Roman cultural groups, while simultaneously controlling the number admitted. And it maximized both the acculturation of learners and their differentiation from one another, producing a pool of people who shared a common sense and a common criteria of greekness or romanness but who were placed in a hierarchy according to their cultural achievements.[53]

Beyond enculturation and stratification, the increasing use of writing in the Roman period also began to play a larger role in the maintenance and distribution of power.[54] One of the primary instruments utilized by the Roman state to implement and safeguard its power over its subjects was the written law. As Hopkins explains:

> The Roman government supplemented taxation with coercion and persuasion. The instruments of coercion, which helped maintain the Roman government and the elite in power were, for example, written laws, courts of justice, bureaucratic administration, and the army. . . . But the system of justice, the adherence to written law, to the precedents of previous decisions, and the reliance on writ-

ten petitions, all symptomised the spread of the Roman
legal system, over the whole Mediterranean basin.[55]

Hopkins also points out that one likely reason for the growth
of literacy during the Roman period was that Roman subjects
were being confronted by, and themselves confronting, Roman
power though writing: "Subjects wrote petitions, and did so in
amazing numbers. They learnt the language of the conquerors
in order to borrow the conqueror's power and to help protect
themselves from exploitation."[56] Even so, Hopkins cautions,
"I am not claiming here that the number of literates exceeds
Harris' estimates, but I am trying to explain why the Roman
conquest state helped produce more literates than ever before."[57]
Thus, even with a limited degree of legal power available to
Roman subjects, we must not overlook the reality that writing
enabled the Roman elite to limit access to their ranks, acculturate
and control conquered peoples, heavily tax and police the underclass, and thus maintain the status quo. As a tool available primarily to the elite, literacy allowed those in power, quite literally,
to write the "rules of the game."

Mary Beard has argued that writing during the Roman period
also played a critical role in defining religious communities and
power relations within them. Even though Roman pagan religious
traditions still relied heavily—even primarily—on oral expression and transmission, "the simple fact, for example, that writing
becomes used, even by a tiny minority, to define the calendar of
rituals or sacred law inevitably changes the nature of the religion
concerned."[58] Specifically, literacy becomes one of the mediums
through which devotees record, safeguard, and gain access to
divine revelation and instruction. One significant effect of this
development is that the religious community then begins to
privilege those who have access to that written tradition—the
literate. Thus, Beard argues that literacy served a pivotal role in
the development of a religious elite within paganism and a proliferation of religious texts that persons among this elite alone
were deemed qualified to access.

This growing ideological dominance of the elite is particularly clear in the history of the various collections of priestly books. These books were not static or fixed. They came over time to incorporate more and more religious decisions and precedents—presumably often in conflict with one another. This proliferation of decision-making, in its turn, came to demand a whole set of higher-level rules and higher-level religious "experts" to offer authoritative interpretation of the otherwise confusing mass of conflicting data, men of the elite who (unlike the majority) could assert their claim to "understand the system."[59]

Of course, similar claims could be made for Judaism during the Roman era (as with Christianity in the late Roman period). As noted earlier, Judaism prior to and throughout the Roman period became heavily dependent on written tradition for the preservation and dissemination of its religious doctrine. Priests and scribes served as those experts who mediated and expounded on the Law and Prophets for the rest of the people.[60] Indeed, we must be careful not to make assumptions about their motives. Power does not always corrupt! Common sense tells us that there were likely a number of priests and scribes—both pagan and Israelite—who were motivated primarily by the drive for self-aggrandizement, while others made a sincere attempt to relate the tradition in ways that they believed led the people more deeply into God's (or the gods') blessing. Perhaps most of the religious elite were driven by a mix of these motivations in varying degrees. In any case, however, the use of the written word as an authoritative repository of tradition, among other factors (such as heredity), guarded access to that tradition. Thus, literacy's facilitation of social stratification and control in Roman society as a whole could be found in its religious systems as well, pagan and Israelite. And in the case of both religious systems, it led to a system of polity that restricted access to divine revelation and granted the authority to mediate that revelation to the elite.

Summary

The aim of this chapter has been to explore the state and function of literacy in the Greco-Roman world in the centuries leading up to and including Luke's composition of his gospel and Acts. This, as I noted in the introduction, is to be one of our primary considerations as we explore Luke's social location. What we have found, leaning on those who are familiar with the relevant data, is that literacy, while increasing in the centuries prior to Luke, was still likely limited to no more than 10 percent of the population by the start of the Christian era. Among this literate minority, far fewer still excelled to the point of studying, let alone mastering, grammar and rhetoric. While there were undoubtedly exceptions to the rule, lack of access to educational instruction, economic limitations, and the embrace of "limited good" among the peasant majority likely prevented nearly all among their ranks from achieving even a basic level of literacy. In contrast, some among the social elite embraced literacy and displays of literary acumen as a way of gaining honor from their peers. They also employed literacy as a means of introducing other socially and economically advantaged persons to Greco-Roman culture and the rules of social stratification. Moreover, the written word served as mechanism for social control, inscribing civil law and divine revelation and placing the authority to interpret and enforce those traditions in the hands of an elite few.

CHAPTER 2

Luke's Literary Artistry

As stated in the introduction, one of the main objectives of the work is to offer an informed assessment of Luke's social location using literacy as a primary index. Two tasks taken up in these pages are geared toward making this determination. The first, which was engaged in the preceding chapter, is to determine what levels of literacy were common to which social strata in the Mediterranean world and Roman Palestine. The second, pursued here in this chapter, is to determine Luke's level of literacy.

To readers familiar with Luke's major contribution to the Christian canon (Luke and Acts take up more than one quarter of the New Testament), it may seem unnecessary to spend much time and space dwelling on the matter of Luke's literary acumen. Luke is commonly regarded—at least among relatively recent interpreters—as one of the most gifted and erudite writers of the NT, and his literary artistry is celebrated by many a reader. Based on this common perception, we may be tempted to skip the formal analysis and simply rush to the conclusion that Luke's work shows him to be very highly educated, suggesting in turn that Luke was among the elite. Indeed, the following discussion will do little to discourage this conclusion. Nevertheless, trudging through the following material is useful for at least two reasons. First, a variety of readers will (I hope) make use of this book, and many of them may not be all that familiar with Luke's writing. It will be important for them to engage at least some elements of Luke's literary artistry as they assess the argument I am promoting. Second, the following analysis will endeavor to show the extent to which Luke made use of and mastered literary and rhetorical conventions of his time. Even for readers familiar with Luke-Acts, this will perhaps serve as a useful clarification and confirmation of what many already sense to be true about the evangelist's writings.

Although the entirety of the chapter is devoted to this task, we will still need to be selective in the material we engage. What I discuss below is a sampling of Luke's literary abilities, most of which have close parallels in other ancient writers of his literary milieu, and others that on their own terms reveal Luke's literary creativity and competence.

Mastery of Greek and Stylistic Range

Readers of Luke familiar with Greek commonly point out that Luke's proficiency with the language is the most advanced among the gospel writers, and perhaps even among the rest of the NT writers (with the possible exception of Hebrews). Assuming that Luke used Mark's gospel as a source for his own, commentators note the many grammatical and syntactical improvements Luke makes to the material he borrows from the earlier gospel.[1] Beyond his grammatical proficiency, Luke's vocabulary is wide-ranging, far more so than the other gospel writers.[2] H. J. Cadbury compared Luke's vocabulary to Attic Greek prose writers, classical poets, and later Greek writers, noting many similarities and concluding that Luke's use of the language comes closest of all the NT writings to that of writers from the classical period.[3] Hans Conzelmann notes many points of contact between Luke's style and vocabulary and the historians Josephus, Plutarch, and Lucian.[4] François Bovon argues that although the evangelist writes in *Koine*, the Greek of Hellenistic and Roman times, and not in the Attic of classical writers, "Luke attempts to find a middle path between the vernacular, which one finds in Mark or nonliterary papyri, and the artificial Greek of reform movements, such as the Atticizing fashion of the second century."[5] Fitzmyer is among many in concluding that Luke's elevated style was "determined in part by his desire to write his account in the mold of contemporary Hellenistic literary composition."[6]

Another feature of Luke-Acts that supports Fitzmyer's contention is the prologues to both volumes.

> Since many have undertaken to set down an orderly account of the events that have been fulfilled among us, just as they were handed on to us by those who from the beginning were eyewitnesses and servants of the word, I too decided, after investigating everything carefully from the very first, to write an orderly account for you, most excellent Theophilus, so that you may know the truth concerning the things about which you have been instructed. (Luke 1:1-4)

> In the first book, Theophilus, I wrote about all that Jesus did and taught from the beginning until the day when he was taken up to heaven, after giving instructions through the Holy Spirit to the apostles whom he had chosen. (Acts 1:1-2)

The structure and vocabulary of the prologue reveal numerous parallels with the prologues of other ancient works. As helpfully summarized by Bovon:

> Writing in the genre of the prologue, ancient writers would typically mention their predecessors and give an assessment of their work; then they would emphasize the quality of their information (eye-witness observation and firsthand research) and the arrangement of the treatise; and last, they would make a few statements about their own person and

> literary purpose. A dedication was often added. . . . The
> prologue applied to the entire work, but each successive
> volume would also have a smaller, less pretentious pro-
> logue, which would make reference to the previous volume
> and specify the contents of the next.[7]

Scholars have debated the precise genre of Greco-Roman writing to which Luke's prologue is most closely aligned (the "scientific tradition," biography, or historiography).[8] It is clear, however, that prologues in antiquity sharing common elements were utilized in several genres, and the overall shape and narrative aim of Luke-Acts strongly suggests that it corresponds most closely to the rather loose and variable genre of historiography while containing elements of biography.[9] For our purposes, however, it is sufficient to note the elevated style and conventional features of the prologue that place it in the company of other advanced Greco-Roman writing. Beyond the features summarized by Bovon above, we should also note that the prologue to the gospel is a single, long sentence, containing what is called a "periodic structure," comprised of a "protasis" in vv. 1-2 ("Since many have undertaken") and an "apodosis" in vv. 3-4 ("I too decided, after investigating everything"). These verses contain the following, carefully composed, parallel framework:

a Since many have undertaken (1:1a)

   b to set down an orderly account (1:1b)

      c just as they were handed down to us (1:2)

a I too decided (1:3a)

   b to write an orderly account (1:3b)

      c so that you may know the truth (1:4)[10]

Based on Luke's preface and the parallels she finds in the "scientific tradition" in Luke's day, Loveday Alexander concludes that Luke writes at a "middlebrow" social and cultural level rather than at the level of the literary elite.[11] She is followed by Vernon K. Robbins in this assessment.[12] Other, scholars, such as Fitzmyer, argue that the prologue is an example of "stylistic excellence" that stands out for its formality. It also shows that had he wished, "Luke could have written the Jesus-story in cultivated, literary Greek."[13]

Interestingly, however, Luke chose not to do so. Most of his gospel and Acts is written in his "normal style," the elevated yet not overly formalized Greek noted by Bovon above. Yet, beginning already in 1:5, Luke switches to still another style of Greek containing phrasing and vocabulary that would have reminded readers of Greek translations of the Israelite Scriptures. (For a rough analogy, think of a modern writer suddenly launching into a "King James" style of English.) Coupled with the central focus of his narrative—to present "the things fulfilled among us" (Luke 1:1)—the intent of this stylistic creativity is clear. Luke wants his readers/listeners to see his narrative of the "events fulfilled among us" (1:1) as the continuation of the story recorded in his sacred writings. Luke uses his impressive stylistic range for his rhetorical-theological ends: the stories of Elizabeth and Zechariah, Mary and Joseph, and their children, John and Jesus, are of a piece with the story of God's dealings with God's people, Israel. In fact, these stories are its climax.

Luke's stylistic variation continues in Acts, further demonstrating Luke's mastery over grammatical convention. According to Charles Talbert:

> In the Acts also the writer chooses the style which is suitable for the different periods, places, and persons he is describing. He imitates the LXX [Septuagint—a Greek translation of the Jewish Scriptures] in the first part of Acts and in his missionary speeches to Jews due to his feel for the Palestinian context of the earliest church. His speeches also employ old titles for Jesus and ancient kerygmatic formulae in accord with the archaizing tendency of antiquity. At other times, less solemn, the writer is capable of "painting a scene easily and expansively, dwelling lovingly on the details, in almost conversational tones." Luke simply varies his style in terms of the situation he is depicting and the

tone the situation requires. Indeed, it is the opinion of
H. J. Cadbury that Luke's sensitivity to style is even more
far-reaching than that of the literary men of antiquity who
understood the imitation of classical modes of style.[14]

Literary Conventions

Beyond his grammatical acumen and stylistic range, Luke also
employs a number of conventions common to his literary milieu.
Prefaces, as already noted, are one such convention. In addition,
Luke utilizes a host of literary devices found in Greco-Roman
historiography and biography, including Israelite historiography.

1) *Infancy Narratives* (see Luke 1–2)

In Greco-Roman biography, it was common for writers to
include stories of the main figure's birth and early years,
focusing on events and discourse that revealed the subject's
character, special abilities, and calling. Similar to their typical
function in his literary milieu, Luke employs his birth stories
to unveil one of his main characters, Jesus. But Luke significantly modifies the convention by expanding its focus and
function. He also uses infancy narrative to introduce us to the
character of John. In fact, Luke intertwines accounts of their
annunciations and births to compose a "step-parallelism"
between the two characters (see below). Moreover, the infancy
narratives include several other characters, and it is largely
through their character speech that we learn the broad contours of the long-awaited salvation Luke announces and de-
picts in the pages to follow (see below). Thus, Luke broadens
the typical purview of infancy narrative, using it not only to
shape our understanding of a single character but also to
serve as a rich and compelling introduction to God's plan of
deliverance portrayed in Luke-Acts as whole, highlighting
the main motifs that course throughout the rest of his two-
volume work.

2) *Birth Announcements* (see Luke 1:5-25; 26-38)

Found in Israel's Scriptures (see Gen 16:7-12 [Ishmael]; Gen 17:1-8; 18:1-15 [Isaac]; and Judg 13:1-23 [Samson]), birth announcements are formal literary forms that typically contain the following elements[15]:

1. The appearance of an angel of the Lord (or appearance of the Lord)

2. Fear or prostration of the visionary confronted by this supernatural appearance

3. The divine message:
   a. The visionary is addressed by name
   b. A qualifying phrase describing the visionary
   c. The visionary is urged not to be afraid
   d. A woman is with child or is about to be with child
   e. She will give birth to the (male) child
   f. The name by which the child is to be called
   g. An etymology interpreting the name
   h. The future accomplishments of the child (see below)

4. A response from the recipient

5. The giving of a sign to reassure the visionary

Beyond these formal elements, birth announcements sometimes give an indication of the child's character and role with respect to God's people. Luke also employs them for this purpose, using them to inform his readers of how John and Jesus fit into the advent of God's kingdom.

3) *Genealogies* (see Luke 3:23-38)

Common in biblical and Hellenistic writing, genealogies served a variety of purposes. The evangelist's use of the genealogy in Luke 3 parallels two of its functions in Israel's Scriptures: (1) to establish the kinship relations between important characters and (2) to set the present matters at hand in relation to the larger history of the relationship between God and God's people. Luke's genealogy not only demonstrates Jesus' descent from David, thereby reinforcing the claim that Jesus is the Messiah, but also promotes the universal perspective of Luke-Acts by tracing Jesus' lineage all the way back to Adam.

4) *Travel Accounts*
(see Luke 9:51–19:44; Acts 12:25–21:16; 27:1–28:6)

Travel accounts in ancient narratives took several forms, though at times these forms were combined: the "march," or inland expedition, often recounted military campaigns (e.g., Herodotus, the Pentateuch); the "travel description" described land travel, taking an interest in geography and ethnography; the "sea travel account" focused on coastal voyages.[16] Luke, who makes use of both the march and sea travel forms, uses travel accounts to accomplish at least three narrative or rhetorical ends. First, Luke employs the travel sections and journey theme to unify the otherwise episodic character of his gospel as well as to unify the narrative of Luke-Acts as a whole. From Luke 9 onward, the reader is repeatedly reminded that Jesus and his disciples are "on the way" *toward* Jerusalem. For it is in this sacred city that pivotal events of Jesus' ministry will take place: betrayal, arrest, crucifixion, and resurrection (see 9:51; 18:31-33). And it is *from* here, as depicted in Acts, that the message of salvation will spread to the ends of the earth as Jesus' followers take up his journey as their own (see Acts 1:8). Thus, the narrative as a whole is united by this movement toward and then away from the sacred city. Second, Luke uses the journey motif to emphasize the missionary character of discipleship. Disciples of Jesus are depicted as those who leave their homes behind and follow after Jesus to Jerusalem and beyond (e.g., 9:23-27, 57-62; 10:1-12). And it is on this journey to Jerusalem, from

Luke 9 onward, that the disciples repeatedly receive instruction on what it means both to embrace the kingdom and to serve as its stewards. The journey theme continues in Acts, as the followers of Jesus—empowered by the Spirit—now take the lead in witnessing to and mediating God's salvation to others in an ever-expanding arc away from Jerusalem, fulfilling their calling to "be my witnesses in Jerusalem, in all Judea and Samaria, and to the ends of the earth" (Acts 1:8). For this reason, the church receives the nickname of "the Way" (see Acts19:9, 23; 22:4; 24:14, 22—*ho hodos*). Third, the journey theme also assists Luke in portraying the centrality of Jerusalem in God's plan of salvation. In so presenting his two-volume work and shaping the travel narratives in this fashion, Luke provides a structure and plot to his narrative that unify his work while emphasizing the rootedness of God's deliverance of humankind in Jerusalem and God's relationship with Israel.

5) *Embedded Letters* (see Acts 15:23-29; 23:26-30)

In historical narrative, letters were frequently employed to provide commentary on the events in focus and to lend authenticity and verisimilitude to the account.[17] Two such letters appear in Acts (Acts 15:23-29 and 23:26-30), both of which closely correspond to Hellenistic epistolary form. The first records and communicates the judgment of the apostles and elders during their conference in Jerusalem. Opening with a periodic sentence in elevated Greek style (15:24-26), the letter functions as a decree of sorts announcing the council's decision regarding whether Gentiles need to be circumcised and abstain from unclean foods. As such, it affirms the resolution of the conflict on which the immediate narrative has focused and further promotes the themes of inclusion and faithful community deliberation that are central to Luke's account. The second letter is from the tribune, Claudius, to the governor, Felix, explaining why he is sending Paul to the governor.

It too is directly connected to the surrounding narrative and captures well the themes of conflict, the vicious response of Paul's detractors, and Paul's innocence.

6) *Parallelism and Patterning*

Ancient historians frequently composed patterns in their narration of both characters and events, with the result that events and persons were in some fashion compared to one another. Clear examples are found in Homer's *Iliad* and *Odyssey*, the plays of Aeschylus and Euripides, the histories of Herodotus and Thucydides, and in Virgil's *Aeneid*, *Eclogues*, and *Georgics*, among others.[18] According to Charles Talbert, who has offered one of the more detailed surveys of this technique in ancient historiography and Luke-Acts, such patterns could function as "(a) an assist to the memory of the readers/hearers, that is, a mnemonic device; (b) an assist to the meaning of the whole or of a section; or (c) as abstract architectonic principle, a convention, used solely for aesthetic purposes."[19] Luke makes use of a wide array of patterning and parallelism. While not precluding the possibility that Luke used the device to assist readers' memories and for aesthetic reasons, it appears that Luke's primary aim was to draw comparisons between characters and their actions in order to advance his rhetorical and theological ends.

For most of his infancy narrative, Luke presents the births and early days of John and Jesus in parallel fashion. First, we encounter the announcement of John's birth (1:5-25), then that of Jesus (1:26-38). Next we hear Elizabeth's exclamation of joy (1:41-45), then that of Mary (1:46-56). This is followed by the pairing of John's birth and Zechariah's hymn of praise (1:57-80) with Jesus' birth and the proclamation of the heavenly host (2:1-20). Commentators frequently note that one of the clear implications of Luke's parallel accounts of John and Jesus is that it is comparative, with the result that Jesus emerges as the more exalted of the two. The instances of "step-parallelism" created by these correspondences consist of the following:

1. John the Baptist is great before the Lord (1:15a), but Jesus is "great" and "holy" without qualification (1:32, 35).

2. John the Baptist is filled with the Holy Spirit even from his mother's womb (1:15c), but the very conception of Jesus involves a creative act of God through the Holy Spirit (1:35b).

3. John the Baptist will make ready for the Lord a prepared people (1:17e), but Jesus will actually rule over the house of Jacob/Israel and possess a kingdom without end (1:33). Furthermore, Jesus himself is to be called "Lord" (1:43, 76; 2:11) and "Savior" (2:11), designations typically reserved for Yahweh in Israelite tradition.

4. John is consecrated to Nazarite abstinence, but Jesus' holiness as the divine son extends to the very basis of his existence.

While most commentators are content to see the function of the device as simply to display Jesus' superiority over John, I think much more is at work here. In my view, the cooperative (rather than competitive) tone dominating Luke's portrayal of the two figures, the emphasis on both John and Jesus as persons essential to the accomplishment of God's awaited advent, and the fact that Luke presents John as readying Israel for the advent of Yahweh *and* Jesus together point to a much more sophisticated function for the step-parallelism Luke employs. Together, these elements of Luke's portrayal suggest that Luke is primarily concerned to portray the greatness of Jesus neither vis-à-vis John, who some may have thought is the Messiah, nor vis-à-vis John as the representative of the Period of Israel, but vis-à-vis John as one who *prepares the way of the Lord*.[20] This proposal helps us grasp two important functions served by the step-parallelism Luke composes between John and Jesus. First, it is Jesus' superior greatness and significance with respect to John as revealed in the step-parallelism

Luke employs that sets him apart as the one for whom John prepares. Otherwise, Jesus' role in the unfolding of God's salvation becomes unclear: i.e., if John prepares the way of the Lord God—and not that (also) of Jesus—then how does Jesus, who is greater than John and who is hailed Messiah and Son of God, fit into God's plan of restoration? By his portrayal of Jesus as greater than John, Luke implies that Jesus must be the one whose way John readies. At the same time, the seeming contradiction that this implication creates (how can John be directly said to prepare the way of the Lord God [see 1:15-16], while it is clearly implied by the narrative that it is Jesus for whom John prepares?) invites Luke's audience to consider that Yahweh's awaited advent and Jesus' coming are somehow one and the same.[21] It also invites Luke's audience to reflect on the nature of the relationship between Jesus and God.

Second, the descriptions of Jesus' significance and person provided by Luke's characters not only provide a point of comparison between Jesus and John, *they are also the very details that suggest a convergence of mission and person between Jesus and God.* Thus, in the case of the paired annunciations, it is crucial to note that the attributes of Jesus' person provided by Luke ("Son of God," conceived by the Holy Spirit, "great," "holy," "Lord," and "Savior") and the description of his mission (will reign on Jacob's throne *forever*) do not simply serve to reveal the superiority of Jesus (and thus imply that Jesus is also—somehow—the one for whom John prepares). Just as important, they are what cast Jesus in a manner that presents him as no mere mortal. They further lead Luke's audience to perceive that *Jesus'* coming fulfills *Yahweh's* awaited advent. In other words, Jesus is not simply greater than John and thus the one for whom John prepares. Jesus is greater than John and the one for whom John prepares because he represents Yahweh in his mission and person.

There are also numerous parallels Luke composes between Luke and Acts and also within Acts, especially between Jesus and Paul (similar journeys, miracles, trials, even passion

predictions), Jesus and Peter (similar miracles and bold proclamation of the gospel), Jesus and Stephen (Stephen's review
of history and death, including the line, "Lord, do not hold
this sin against them" [Acts 7:60; cf. Luke 23:34]), and Peter
and Paul (similar miracles of healing). Here too the patterning
and parallelism is not simply for show but to advance Luke's
rhetorical-theological ends. The connections Luke draws between these characters serves as another demonstration that
the mission of Jesus begun in the gospel is now continuing
in the ministry of his followers in Acts. It also serves to under-
score the unity of the early church's mission, including that
of Paul and Peter.

7) *Remembrance, Citation, and Allusion*

One pervasive feature of Israelite writing is the remembrance of, citation of, and allusion to its sacred tradition.
Israel's Scriptures frequently hearken back to earlier stories,
calling their readers to remember monumental events of their
past, to color a present event in the hue of a former one, to
situate the present moment within the history of God's dealings with Israel, or to call to mind Yahweh's instruction on
what it means to be God's people. Sometimes this is done in
obvious form. At other times the connections are more subtly
drawn: a turn of phrase; a description of present events that
remind readers of events long ago; key words, such as "com-
passion," "steadfast love," "Egypt," or "Abraham" that represent essential strands of the Israelite worldview. Luke, along
with the other evangelists, is a master at this form of remembrance, weaving into his account references both subtle and
direct to this ancient story as he narrates its continuation in
Jesus. To take an example, consider Luke's presentation of
Elizabeth and Zechariah at the start of his infancy narrative.
We have already noted above that Luke switches from the
elevated, literary Greek of the prologue (1:1-4) to a style of
Greek reminiscent of Greek translations of Israel's Scriptures.

The point of this seems to be Luke's intent to present his gospel as the continuation of these Scriptures, their "next chapter," if you will. Reinforcing this effect, readers familiar with the Old Testament (OT) will likely catch the echoes of Abraham and Sarah in Luke's description of Zechariah and Sarah as a devout, elderly couple who have been barren for long years, only to find out in their old age that they will conceive and birth a son who will play a pivotal role in the realization of God's promises to Israel. The rest of the infancy narrative participates in this manifold remembrance of the "days of old," with additional allusions to familiar stories (such as the story of Hannah, Elkanah, and Samuel in the accounts of John's and Jesus' births) and hymns that are a collage of OT phrases, themes, and references to God's promises. In doing so, Luke brings the past into the present, or, perhaps better said, casts the present events as of a piece with what God has done in the past and what God had promised God would do in the future.

Character Speech and Plot Development

There are two additional literary conventions employed by Luke to which I would like to draw your attention: Luke's use of "character speech" (direct and indirect discourse) and plotting (Luke's arrangement of his narrative). Because it is difficult to discuss Luke's use of these two devices separate from the other and because I will elaborate on them in a bit more detail than with the conventions already discussed, I will treat them together here in a distinct section.

The use of direct and indirect discourse was a common feature of ancient historiography, both Greco-Roman and Israelite. It was employed for a variety of purposes: to dramatize the motivations leading to a moment of decision, to entertain, to characterize key figures, to inform the reader of details not expressed in the third-person narration, to display rhetorical artistry, or any combination of these. In addition to these functions, direct speech in ancient historical narrative often serves to present the historian's own perspective on the matters he records.

The "interpretive" use of character speech among ancient historians is manifested in several different ways. In much ancient historiography, direct discourse is utilized to focus attention on key events or situations and to interpret their significance within the context of the historical account in which they occur. Character speech is also commonly employed in both Israelite and Greco-Roman historiography to repeat and emphasize certain themes throughout an account, with the effect that the narrative is unified under a set of motifs that reflect what the writer considers to be the most noteworthy elements of the history recorded. For instance, in Israelite historiography, key motifs are often gathered into lengthy discourses that are placed at crucial turning points in the narrative, either to review what has come before it, to preview what is yet to be narrated, or both (e.g., Exod 15:1-18; Deut 1:6–4:40; Josh 24:2-15; 2 Sam 6; 7:18-29; 1 Kgs 8:14-53; 2 Chr 13:4-12; 15:1-70). The action of the narrative pauses, a leading character steps forward and offers a (sometimes lengthy) summary of the relationship between God and God's people Israel, and situates the present matters at hand within that story, not unlike a leading character offering a soliloquy in a Shakespearean play. In doing so, these instances of character speech present major portions of the account, or even the entire narrative, under a single, though somewhat complex, vision of God and Israel's relationship with Yahweh.

In Greco-Roman historiography, especially in the works of Herodotus and Thucydides, the actual content of the character speech reported may not directly reflect the views of the writer, but the direct speech still serves a crucial role in the writer's presentation of universal, historical processes leading to the occurrence of the events or circumstances in view. In other words, the presentation of character speech intentionally and thoughtfully recreates a dynamic that represents the writer's interpretive stance on the nature of reality. Later historians, such as Dionysius (first century BCE) and the first-century CE Roman historians Livy and Tacitus, are often cited as those who made copious use of character speech, casting it according to current rhetorical standards.[22] For our purposes, however, it is important to note that at least in the cases of Livy, Tacitus, and Polybius, the intent behind their reproduction of speeches was not merely stylistic or ornamental. For Livy, the speeches not only helped create a dramatic atmosphere but also served to "distill and dramatize a situation's essence" or "to mark and emphasize a critical part in the narrative."[23] Livy's shaping of his speeches also played an essential role in presenting large sections of his narrative according to his own particular conception of the history he records. As Norma P. Miller observes:

> The high point for creative and interpretive speech in Livy is in Books xxi–xxx, his account of the Hannibalic war. It was a crucial period in Rome's history, from which she emerged triumphant; it abounded in exciting events and interesting personalities; and it existed in admirable source material in the history of Polybius. Fortunately for us, most of it still exists in that form, so that we can see what Livy has done with his source. The expansion or contraction, elaboration and reorganization, is here not merely a turning of Polybian Greek into Livian Latin, but an integral part of Livy's presentation of the history of the period.[24]

Tacitus also shaped and composed speeches according to rhetorical convention. But again, a number of scholars have found that a primary interest of Tacitus in his selection, shaping, and arrangement of character speech was to provide moral instruction through characterization and to expound important themes.[25] Similarly, Polybius (second century BCE), who chastises others for composing speeches with little concern for what was actually said, also engaged in the practice of shaping speech material to draw out what he considered to be the chief significance of the events he recorded. Although scholars generally regard Polybius as one of the more faithful recorders of his sources, "like Thucydides before him he shapes and rephrases his material so that the result takes on a decidedly personal coloring."[26] Equally revealing are Polybius' own statements concerning the function of the speeches: "The whole *genus* of orations . . . may be regarded as summaries of events and as the unifying element in historical writing."[27] While certainly not an admission of fabrication (an impropriety for which he immediately proceeds to castigate Timaeus), Polybius' comments show his participation in the common practice of selecting and arranging speeches (whether authentic or not) in order to provide the desired interpretation of events (in the form of summaries) and to unify the narrative under a particular conception of the history recorded.

This same practice of using character speech to emphasize the importance of certain events and to interpret their significance within the history being presented continues in the writings of later Israelite historians, such as Josephus and the writer of 2 Maccabees. In 2 Maccabees, speeches are commonly employed to announce the fundamental theological theme of the work: that the events of Israelite history show God at work caring for God's people, rewarding the faithful and punishing the impious.[28] Moreover, the speeches of the seven brothers martyred for their faith carry the theological focus of the work a step further by indicating that with the death of the martyrs the Lord's anger against Israel might be ended.[29] Josephus, writing in the first century CE, is said to have fabricated speeches "with a particular lavishness."[30] Pere Varneda claims that Josephus stands in the tradition of rhetorically shaped speeches and engages in the common Greco-Roman practice of including speeches at significant moments in the narrative.[31] H. St. John Thackeray also speaks of the "great 'set' speeches inserted at cardinal turning-points in the narrative."[32] Such speeches are "oratorical displays, subserving the general propagandist purpose of the work." They are put into the mouths of the Israelite leaders, such as Agrippa and Eleazar "who must themselves be made to pronounce their impotence and righteous doom."[33] Similarly, B. Gärtner adds that Josephus "makes very free with the principle of putting speeches into the mouths of leading figures," noting also that though at times he is faithful to his sources, "the elaboration of the material is his own."[34] Citing the pair of speeches delivered by Herod and the Emperor (*Jewish War* 1:373-98) he states that "the speeches are means by which the author gives his view of the events."[35]

Many who have studied Luke's presentation of speeches in Acts against this background conclude that Luke, like historians before and contemporary to him, utilized the words of his characters to interpret the significance of key events or situations recorded in the narrative.[36] Among them, Marion Soards has offered one of the more detailed treatments. His work has demonstrated that the speeches in Acts were shaped by the evangelist to articulate the significance of important events and to present a worldview that governed his work as a whole. According to Soards, Luke utilized the repetition of speech to unify what was otherwise a diverse and even incoherent collection of materials into "a history that was coherent, and moreover, ideologically pointed—a history that could, in turn, move through the future selectively preserving the tradition it repeated and thereby deliberately advancing its causes."[37] Soards explains that this repetition of speech as well as the repetition of characteristic elements of the speeches together create the dynamic of *analogy*: "precisely because there are so many speeches in Acts, one is able to compare and contrast the different speeches with each other to notice where and how language, motifs, and patterns are reiterated and varied."[38] He further describes the creation of analogy through repetition as a "deliberative, selective process that gives clues to the real meaning of the narrative."[39] Soards argues that when the speeches are examined collectively with the dynamic of analogy in mind, one finds that "Luke weaves speeches into the narrative of Acts and creates emphasis so that the speeches articulate a distinct worldview."[40] Thus, Luke not only utilizes the speeches to interpret the significance of particular events, but through the consistent repetition of particular elements presents an ideological context in which the narrative as a whole is to be viewed.

Less commonly recognized is that Luke employs character speech in his gospel for the very same purposes. In my doctoral dissertation, I examined Luke's use of direct and indirect discourse in his infancy narrative and Luke 24.[41] I argued that through the consistent repetition of six dimensions, or motifs, in the words of his characters at the beginning of the gospel, the evangelist introduces a distinct ideological context, or worldview, that is to guide his audience's understanding of the narrative to follow. The saving events Luke records:

(a) are the result of God's sovereignty and saving plan to bring them to pass

(b) mark the eschatological fulfillment of God's promises

(c) culminate in the restoration of Israel and all humanity

(d) are to be met with faith, rejoicing, and witness

(e) are carried out by Jesus, the divine son, whose arrival is presented as God's awaited advent

(f) are characterized by their reversal of human customs, expectations and efforts to thwart God's plan of salvation

These same motifs and the same ideological context they together form is reasserted once again in the character speech of Luke 24.

Concentrated at the start and close of the gospel, direct and indirect discourse unique to Luke also plays a key role in the structuring, or plotting, of his two-volume work. As I just stated, Luke 24, primarily through character speech, rehearses the ideological context presented in Luke 1–2 (represented by the list of motifs provided above). But Luke also integrates the major themes that dominate the gospel narrative *following* the infancy narrative into this final chapter as he portrays their continuing development and transformation in light of the reality of the resurrection (also primarily through character speech). These major themes of his gospel include:

(1) the divine necessity and scriptural fulfillment of Jesus' suffering, death, and resurrection

(2) the rejection of Jesus

(3) the misunderstanding of the disciples

(4) journeying as mission

(5) Jesus' ministry in the power of the Spirit

(6) table fellowship with Jesus as a symbol of life in the kingdom

From the vantage point of Luke 24, we are in a position to see how the themes that were central to Luke's preceding narrative not only converge in this final chapter but also, in their transformation, become increasingly intertwined with one another. The resolution of the *disciples' misunderstanding* (3) hinges on their finally grasping *the divine and scriptural necessity of Jesus suffering, death, and resurrection* (1) and the saving significance of these events, including *Jesus' rejection* (2) by Israelite and Gentile alike. Moreover, the disciples' faithful embrace of the reality of the resurrection and its significance is enabled not only by Jesus opening the Scriptures to them (vv. 32, 45) but by their *table fellowship* (6), now with the *risen* Christ (vv. 33, 41-43). Through their proclamation of these events to others, culminating in their commissioning as witnesses (vv. 48-49), the disciples embark on another *journey of mission* (4), themselves empowered by *Jesus' ongoing ministry in the power of the Spirit* (5).

At the same time that the evangelist skillfully recasts and interlaces the major ideas of the preceding narrative, he also shapes his character speech to recall the ideological context he established in the opening chapters. Luke does not do this obtrusively. Rather, his recasting of the major plotlines of his gospel in light of the resurrection takes up the dimensions of the ideological context of Luke 1–2. Thus, it is *through* his recasting of the motifs of the preceding narrative—and not so much alongside his portrayal of their transformation—that Luke reemphasizes this worldview. Stated differently, in his final chapter Luke brings the major story lines of the gospel *into alignment* with the vision of salvation introduced in the infancy narrative, and it is the resurrection that makes this alignment possible. Repeated expressions of the divine necessity of Jesus' passion and resurrection and their fulfillment of the Scriptures reflect five of the six dimensions of the evangelist's worldview. More precisely, Luke's fundamental claim that what has come to pass is rooted in *the will and power of God to save* (a) is integral to this motif, as is his portrayal of God's promised salvation in Jesus against a background of *eschatological fulfillment* (b). The risen Jesus' interpretation of these divinely ordained events also emphasizes the notion that *Jesus embodies the visitation of Yahweh in his mission and person* (e) as the exalted Messiah and divine son (vv. 46, 49). The fuller kerygmatic expression of divine necessity and scriptural fulfillment in the final episode of Luke 24 (see vv. 44-47) also incorporates the dimension of *restoration* (c). Here, as in the infancy narrative, Luke announces that God's salvation will consist of the forgiveness of sins and extend to all humankind. Also manifested in Luke's recasting of this motif is the notion of *reversal* (f): the paradoxical reality of the divine son's suffering and God's reversal of the "human no" to Jesus emerges through the repetition of Jesus' passion predictions that have now become *kerygma*. Finally, Luke's presentation of the misunderstanding and journey motifs in light of the resurrection reflects his concern to show that the good news of God's salvation in Jesus is to be embraced with the *faithful response of belief and witness* (d) as a new journey of mission is to be taken by the disciples who now understand (see also vv. 52-53).

Luke's focused re-presentation of the worldview introduced in the infancy narrative—through his recasting of the major motifs of the gospel in light of the resurrection—is likely intended to help his audience discern that the salvation proclaimed at the gospel's beginning is brought to fruition in Jesus' ministry, death, and, above all, his rising from the dead. Thus, Luke 1–2 and 24 provide an interpretive frame for understanding the gospel as a whole, while at the same time the final chapter reveals how the preceding narrative reaches its culmination in Jesus' resurrection. Yet the evangelist's recollection of the ideological context in his closing chapter performs still another function, for the purview of the gospel's end includes not only what has come before it. In the final episode, Jesus' commissioning of his followers as witnesses "from Jerusalem" anticipates the central story line of the evangelist's next volume. Indeed, the central motifs of the gospel, transformed in the blessed aftermath of the resurrection, now go on to propel the narrative of Acts. Consequently, from the vantage point of the gospel's final chapter, Luke's use of character speech serves the function of uniting the narrative of both Luke and Acts under the same multidimensional vision of God's salvation in Jesus.

Use of Rhetorical Patterns and Conventions

Since the early 1980s, biblical scholars have become increasingly interested in how Greco-Roman rhetorical strategies and devices may have been used by the biblical writers, especially the writers of the New Testament (recall that "rhetoric" in this context refers to the "art of persuasion"). Most of the work that has been done in this area has focused on the employment of rhetorical conventions in the NT epistles. Some, however, have also been keeping an eye out for how the writers of biblical narrative may have drawn from this area of study as well. This is an important task. As David Aune points out, "History was not in the curriculum of Greek and Roman schools. Most historians had formal rhetorical education, however, and used that training to write history."[42]

With respect to Luke's two-volume work, a number of scholars have examined Luke's use of rhetorical convention in the speeches of Acts, showing how Luke employed elements of forensic (or "judicial") and deliberative rhetoric. Forensic rhetoric is the style of argumentation associated with the law court, focusing on accusation or defense and making heavy use of proofs. The defense speeches in Acts 22–26 employ this rhetorical style and its attending conventions, as does Paul's speech in Acts 13:16b-41 and Peter's defense before the Sanhedrin in 4:8-12. As noted already in 1980 by William S. Kurz:

> Add to these Lukan examples the many themes especially useful in forensic rhetoric which were mentioned above, such as signs, *tekmēria*, witnesses, written contracts (cf. Scriptures as promises), oaths, oracles (or in Christian terms, prophecies), passionate apologetic stressing Jesus' innocence and the court scenes of Jesus and Paul, and it seems that a fairly strong case for the influence of Hellenistic rhetoric in the writing of Luke-Acts can be made.[43]

Deliberative rhetoric urges listeners to adopt a certain perspective and to act on it. It is the language of exhortation, characteristically appealing to that which is good, beneficial, or faithful, and the avoidance of what is harmful. Jesus' farewell discourse with his disciples in Acts 1:4-11 performs a deliberative function, while Peter's and Paul's missionary speeches (e.g., Acts 2:14-40; 3:11-26; 10:34-43; 13:16-41) contain both judicial and deliberative rhetoric, defending Jesus' innocence, offering proofs that he is the Messiah, and exhorting their audiences to repent and believe.

Recall earlier when discussing Luke's stylistic range we noted that Luke commonly adapted the style of character speech to fit the speaker and audience at hand. The practice of creating a speech with a style befitting the speaker, subject, and occasion was a common exercise in the rhetorical training of Luke's day, a technique taken over (as we have seen) in the writings of Greco-Roman historians. Termed *prosopopaeia*, the art of suiting speeches to a historical, fictional, or stereotypical figure was described in the following way by Lucian in his *How to Write History* (second century CE): "If a person has to be introduced to make a speech, above all let his language suit his person and his subject, and next let these [words] also be as clear as possible.

It is then, however, that you can play the orator and show your eloquence."[44] The practice is also addressed at length by the first-century rhetorician Theon, and surviving exercises in his rhetorical handbook (*progymnasmata*) and that of Hermogenes from the time of Luke show that it was a basic part of rhetorical training. As Kurz notes, "That Luke at least employed the technique with ease is demonstrated by the distinctive coloration he gives to speeches delivered to different audiences: to the Jerusalem Jews in Acts 2 and 3, to the diaspora Jews in Acts 13, and to the pagans in the Acts 17 Areopagus speech."[45]

Kurz also argues that Luke employs the technique of syllogistic reasoning in the form of a "rhetorical enthymeme." When used by Luke, these enthymemes serve as christological proofs in the mouths of his characters, including Jesus and various speakers in Acts. Aristotle was the first, so far as we know, to define syllogistic reasoning and promote it as a basic standard for much rhetorical proof. The syllogism is a form of reasoning that proceeds from necessary and universal premises to necessary conclusions. Its form consists of the following structure:

> All B is A.
> C is B.
> Therefore C is A.

The enthymeme is an instance of syllogistic reasoning in that it "orders all the persuasive evidence and material into premises that lead to persuasive conclusions."[46] Kurz argues that Luke makes frequent use of the device, at times using the full, three-step syllogistic pattern, but often in an abbreviated two-step form. An example he cites of the form in full is from Acts 2:25-32 and 36, which can be structured as follows:

> It was foretold that the Christ would be resurrected from the dead (Acts 2:31)
>
> God raised Jesus from the dead (Acts 2:32)
>
> Therefore, Jesus is the Christ (Acts 2:36)[47]

A shortened form of the same enthymeme is found in Luke's summary of Paul's preaching in Acts 17:2b-3, in which the major premise is stated ("it is necessary for the Christ to suffer and to rise from the dead"), while the minor premise is implied (God raised Jesus), leading to the conclusion, "This Jesus, whom I proclaim to you, is the Christ." Other examples Kurz lists for Luke's "two-step proof" as instances of enthymemes include Luke 24:26-27, 44-48.

The recognition that Luke, as other Greco-Roman historians, was familiar with and utilized rhetorical conventions has become common—though in varying degrees—among interpreters.[48] The conclusion of P. E. Satterthwaite is now shared by many:

> At point after point Acts can be shown to operate according to conventions similar to those outlined in classical rhetorical treatises. There are some aspects which are hard to explain other than by concluding that Luke was aware of rhetorical conventions: the preface; the layout of the speeches; the presentation of the legal proceedings in Acts 24–26. . . . In general, it seems fair to speak of a considerable indebtedness to classical rhetoric; that is, he gives clear indication of having received the kind of (rhetorical) education one would expect of a Greco-Roman writer of this period who embarked on a work of this sort.[49]

At the same time, as Satterthwaite goes on to comment, "Luke is not a slave of classical conventions." Rather, Luke's creative freedom in his handling of these techniques "implies a considerable mastery of those conventions."[50]

Use of Pathos

Still another rhetorical technique that Luke likely employed in his writing, yet one that has been largely neglected by scholars, is his use of pathos as a means of engaging his readers. Greco-

Roman handbooks on rhetoric, beginning with Aristotle and continuing into the first century of the Common Era with Quintilian, commonly identified *pathos* (emotional appeal) alongside *ethos* (appeal to the character of the speaker) and *logos* (use of reason) as the three main forms of rhetorical persuasion.[51] While the comments of ancient rhetoricians apply most directly to the composition of speeches, these and other principles of rhetorical persuasion influenced written discourse as well, such as treatises and letters. Accordingly, many have profitably applied Greco-Roman rhetorical theory to Paul's epistles, with some focusing on Paul's use of *pathos* and *ethos*.[52]

Yet the use of *pathos* was not confined by the ancients to speeches, persuasive treatises, or letters. Aristotle's *Poetics* examines how the dramatic elements of plot, character, and language in Greek tragedy combine to produce the emotional responses of pity and fear. Aristotle claimed that the goal of tragedy—not simply a consequence or ancillary objective, but its goal—is to evoke the emotions of pity and fear in its audience and in doing so to lead the audience to a more complete understanding of those emotions and the nature of life in general. He defines tragedy as follows:

> Tragedy is an imitation of an action that is admirable, complete and possesses magnitude; in language made pleasurable, each of its species separated in different parts; performed by actors, not through narration; effecting through pity and fear the purification (*katharsis*) of such emotions.[53]

Moreover, we also must be careful not to draw a hard-and-fast distinction between rhetorical oratory and narrative form, since the latter was commonly employed in rhetorical discourse. For instance, judicial, or forensic, rhetoric typically included a *narratio* near the beginning of the speech in which the circumstances of the case were relayed to the court. Among Roman rhetoricians, these came to be highly interpreted versions of the "facts" oriented toward the advantage of the speaker's client, with some rhetoricians freely employing emotional appeal to shape audience response. Speaking to this point, Quintilian complains that some among his colleagues neglect this use of affective appeal: "I am therefore all the more surprised at those who hold that there should be no appeal to the emotions in the narration. But why, when I am instructing the judge, should I refuse to move him as well?"[54]

Accordingly, Quintilian, following his mentor, Cicero, emphasized that "there is scope for an appeal to the emotions . . . in every part of a speech" and that "the prime essential for stirring the emotions of others is, in my opinion, first to feel those emotions oneself."[55] Quintilian goes on to describe the technique for eliciting such emotional arousal, one that essentially amounts to dramatic storytelling. Citing Quintilian, Mario DiCicco explains:

> In order to generate these emotions, he uniquely suggests the practice of vivid imagination resulting from "certain experiences which the Greeks call fantasiai, and the Romans *visions*, whereby things absent are presented to our imagination with such extreme vividness that they actually seem to be before our eyes." Through this power of the mind, the orator can visualize the scene and circumstances of a murder, for example, and experience "the blood, the deathly pallor, the groan of agony, the death rattle." In this way, the orator will stir up the appropriate emotions as if one were present at the actual occurrence.[56]

These examples affirm that within Luke's socio-literary milieu the use of emotional appeal for rhetorical effect was common in both nonnarrative and narrative forms of persuasion. To convincingly demonstrate Luke's use of pathos in the construction of his narrative would take us well beyond the confines of this chapter. For that discussion I would refer the reader to *The Heart of Biblical Narrative: Rediscovering Biblical Appeals to the Emotions*.[57] But allow me, for illustrative purposes, to offer an example of Luke's use of pathos for his rhetorical ends in the annunciation of John's birth (Luke 1:5-25).

Luke's use of affective appeal to draw his readers into the story is apparent at numerous points. Several techniques designed to elicit pathos are found here: inviting admiration and sympathy for characters from readers, narrating events that are of utmost importance for the characters involved and also the readers, nostalgic allusion to previous events in the life of God's people, astonishing inversion of the expected, conflict, and ending the passage with a lack of resolution. Let us work through the passage, focusing on how these features accompany and illuminate the basic plotting of the passage and may be meant to affect Luke's audience.

In his impressive commentary on Luke, Joel Green treats vv. 8-23 as a unit distinct from, though closely connected to, vv. 5-7 and vv. 24-25. He further proposes a chiastic structure for vv. 8-23:

(A) Service, Sanctuary, People (vv. 8-10)

    (B) Angel's Appearance and Zechariah's Response
        (vv. 11-12)

      (C) Announcement of "Good News"
          (vv. 13-17; cf. v. 19)

    (B') Zechariah's Objection and Angel's Response
        (vv. 18-20)

(A') People, Sanctuary, and Service

Green notes that the chiastic structure presents "the weight of emphasis falling, as we might expect, on the angelic message concerning John's birth and role in salvation history."[58] Most commentators would concur with this assessment of Luke's emphasis, and it is difficult to argue against it. There may be more than one emphasis in a given passage, however, and the omission of vv. 5-7 and vv. 24-25 from Green's structuring of vv. 8-23 obscures another important element Luke sought to convey in this pericope. Consider now the chiastic structure of the passage with vv. 5-7 and vv. 24-25 included:

(A) Faithful couple, yet barren Elizabeth (vv. 5-7)

  (B) Service, Sanctuary, People (vv. 8-10)

    (C) Angel's Appearance and Zechariah's Response
    (vv. 11-12)

      (D) Announcement of "Good News"
      (vv. 13-17; cf. v. 19)

    (C') Zechariah's Objection and Angel's Response
    (vv. 18-20)

  (B') People, Sanctuary, and Service (vv. 21-23)

(A') Pregnant Elizabeth offers faithful praise (vv. 24-25)

Of course, some may object that the chiasm as I present it does not preserve a balance of parallel elements, since Zechariah is included in the opening element but not in the closing element, where Elizabeth alone appears to give faithful praise and witness. But this imbalance is just my point, and Luke's, I think, as well. The pericope does not end as it began because something has gone wrong to disrupt how it was supposed to go: that is, Zechariah doubted Gabriel's testimony and was rendered mute. Attending to the affective-rhetorical dimensions of the passage helps us to recognize that Zechariah's disappointing doubt is another element of the text Luke wished to emphasize and also helps us to account for the regrettable imbalance, and withheld resolution, readers encounter at the passage's ending.

How does Luke set up readers for the passage's less than satisfactory denouement? Verses 5-7 offer a textbook case of a writer inviting both admiration and sympathy. Zechariah and Elizabeth are both celebrated by Luke as upstanding, God-fearing, righteous children of Israel. For any of his readers with connections to Israelite tradition, including those on the margins of the early Christian movement, the intent of Luke's introduction of the couple is clear: Elizabeth and Zechariah are to be admired. They are the epitome of Torah faithfulness. The quality of their character makes the abruptly introduced plight they face all the more surprising and even distressing.[59] The righteous in Israel's past are usually blessed with offspring. Why is God withholding children from Elizabeth's womb? Thus, not only admiration but also sympathy is invited from the reader. But in the consideration of their plight there is still another reason for the astute reader to admire the couple (as we noted above). "Wait a minute! Where have I heard this story before? That's right, why Zechariah and Elizabeth are just like Abraham and Sarah!" And it is at this point that the reader begins to suspect that something astonishing is going to take place. The elderly, barren couple—just like Abraham and Sarah—is going to be blessed by God with a child. The reader is also likely to suspect that this child, as did Abraham and Sarah's offspring, is going to play a momentous role in the history of God's people.

Filled with this sense of admiration, sympathy, and nostalgia-laden anticipation, the reader then turns to the opening scene of Zechariah in the temple. Once again Zechariah's faithfulness is stressed as he fulfills his priestly duties and is now blessed with the special privilege of offering the incense in the temple. The potential significance of this moment not only for Zechariah but for all Israel is hinted at by Luke's emphatic description: "the *whole* assembly of the people was praying outside" (v. 10; emphasis added). Then an angel appears, as the reader likely expected to happen at some point (recalling birth announcements preserved in Israel's Scriptures), and the good news speaking to matters of extraordinary significance for the righteous couple and Israel is revealed. A son will be born, set apart for God's service, who will "make ready a people prepared for the Lord" (vv. 13-17).

This is indeed a crescendo moment in the story. Sympathetic readers can't help but experience the joy and rejoicing awaiting Zechariah and Elizabeth (vv. 13-14a) as they feel it on their behalf (empathy). But note how Luke affectively ups the rhetorical ante. Readers are also invited by the evangelist to see the joy that God was working in the lives of Zechariah, Elizabeth, and Israel as potentially applying to their own lives as well: for "*many will rejoice at his birth*" (v. 14b; emphasis added). With this the reader is led to wonder how this story is or could be related to his or her own life story: "for I too could be one of the many who celebrate the birth of this extraordinary babe." By inviting readers to admire Zechariah and Elizabeth, to sympathize with their plight, and to rejoice alongside them with the news of their blessing by God (v. 13-14a), Luke leads readers to the very edge of also embracing the *full account* of why this news is so good not only for Zechariah and Elizabeth but also for all the people (vv. 14b-17), including *themselves*.

A kinder writer would allow the reader to bask in the glow of this jubilant, blessed scene for just a bit and gently lead us through its resolution by recounting Zechariah's own joyous response. But Luke is not so kind, at least not here. Instead, he confronts the reader with an astonishing inversion of the expected as the admirable, faithful, and now wonderfully blessed Zechariah *doubts* the heavenly messenger and asks for a sign. "How will I know that this is so?" Then, picking up the narrator's own words from v. 7, he protests "For I am an old man, and my wife is getting on in years" (v. 18). Zechariah's questioning also foregoes any reference to the wider significance of John's birth; his attention is limited only to his and Elizabeth's condition, as though he got stuck on the angel's opening words and failed to hear the rest of the annunciation. Gabriel's rebuke makes it clear that this was not the response for which he was hoping, and we are likely meant to hear it in a solemn yet scathing tone. Zechariah's doubt is an offense to Gabriel's authority and even that of God (v. 19) and is regarded as nothing less than a lack of faith (v. 20). The faithful Zechariah, blameless in his adherence to God's law, is now deemed faithless at the moment when God's will for him is most incredibly, transparently, and engagingly relayed. His son is to be one who "makes ready a people for the Lord." But Zechariah the father, thus far, is not ready for the extraordinary good news Gabriel announces.

On one level, Zechariah's doubt is understandable. This really is unusual news. Even Abraham questioned the workings of the divine promise when years went by and Sarah produced no heir (Gen 15:1-3; see also 17:7) and asked for a covenant commitment from Yahweh when he was told that he would possess the land of Canaan (Gen 15:8).[60] But the writer of Genesis still emphasizes Abraham's trust in God's promise (Gen 15:6). Such is not the case with Zechariah here in Luke. We have been told in Gabriel's opening line that Zechariah has been praying for a son all along (v. 13). Yet he now doubts God's ability to bring it to pass. Elsewhere in the gospel requests for a sign are also—consistently—interpreted negatively (11:16, 29-30; 23:8).[61] Moreover, the attention Luke gives to Zechariah's inability to speak (note the redundancy in v. 22) and the resultant inability of the people to learn of and rejoice in the tremendous good news that has just been announced, further underscores the disappointing character of Zechariah's response. Zechariah's proclamation of the good news—at least for now—has been put on hold. The people discern that a vision has taken place, but so much is left unsaid. Silence and incomprehensible gesturing replace what should have been a raucous celebration, and Zechariah's service ends in quietude. Thus, as we move to the end of the unit, we find Elizabeth alone rejoicing in God's gift of a child (vv. 24-25).

The interruption readers experience in their admiration for Zechariah is jarring. Emotional ambivalence, accentuated with disappointment and even frustration, is the affect that Luke likely intends. The conflict that ensues between Zechariah and Gabriel (and also God) underscores the seriousness of Zechariah's failure to trust and further contributes to the reader's sense of discomfort. What rhetorical purpose would this emotional free-fall serve? At the very moment Luke leads readers to consider that the good news for Elizabeth, Zechariah, and all the people may also be good news for themselves, he provides for them a striking example of disbelief. While Zechariah's faithful service and impeccable adherence to the regulations of the law are sources of admiration, Luke puts his audience on notice that this alone is not sufficient to embrace the eruption of God's salvation in their midst. Another act of faith, consistent with Zechariah and Elizabeth's admirable piety but beyond it, is also needed.

Indeed, the passage ends on a note of praise, and in this there is hope and expectation that the message will spread. But the chorus that should have included many is now comprised of only one. Moreover, Elizabeth offers her praise in seclusion and is at this point unaware that her personal blessing of a child is really good news for all people. The scene thus ends with a lack of resolution, with a priest that has so much to say and tell but whose testimony is silenced by little faith and lack of voice. For many readers, this is unacceptable, and they eagerly await the moment of John's birth when Zechariah might then believe, have his tongue loosed, and offer his belated praise. In subversively shaping the narrative this way, Luke already has readers rooting for the acceptance and proclamation of the good news by the characters in the narrative, thereby preparing "the way of the Lord" within the readers themselves.

Summary

There is much more that we could have done in this chapter to enrich our investigation of Luke's literary artistry. We could have explored the Emmaus pericope in Luke 24 (vv. 13-35), commonly considered a "gem of literary art,"[62] and its display of multiple structuring devices. We could have carefully studied the hymns of the infancy narrative, noting Luke's skillful interweaving of various OT themes and allusions. We could have engaged Luke's casting of Jesus in the mold of Israelite heroes of old, such as Elijah, Moses, and Isaiah, or examined more carefully his shaping of Paul's speeches in Acts.

But I trust that the preceding survey has done enough to show that Luke was intimately familiar with a host of literary devices common to his literary milieu. As we have seen, Luke utilized various conventions and techniques of historical and biographical narration. Among those techniques, several reveal Luke's skillful use of grammar and rhetorical convention. We noted that Luke's Greek is among the best of the NT writers. Moreover, he frequently adapts the style of his Greek to show his literary competence (as in the prologue), for theological ends (as in the infancy narrative), or to follow the rhetorical/historical convention of matching speeches with settings and subjects (*prosopopaeia*). In addition, as did other Hellenistic and Roman historians, Luke employs rhetorical strategies and patterns of argumentation, using the forms of forensic and deliberative rhetoric, the syllogistic pattern of the *enthymeme*, the purposeful shaping of speeches, and *pathos* to guide his audience's affective response. Furthermore, these rhetorical techniques are integrated within and (especially in the case of character speech) marshaled to serve the rather complex plotting of his two-volume work.

The conclusion that emerges from this survey is that Luke clearly received advanced training in both grammar and rhetoric and likely read widely from the Hellenistic literary repertoire, including both Greco-Roman writings and the Israelite sacred tradition with which he was intimately engaged. Not only does Luke demonstrate a familiarity with the literary and rhetorical conventions of his milieu, he also adapts and stretches these conventions to his own ends, revealing an impressive degree of mastery over those devices. While aesthetics are in the eye of the beholder, it is also worth noting, as we did at the start of this chapter, that many readers of Luke and Acts celebrate the artistry with which Luke shapes these conventions and composes his narrative.

CHAPTER 3

Luke the Elite Evangelist

In chapter 1, we examined literacy rates in the Greco-Roman world and in Roman Palestine. What we found was that literacy was confined to a small percentage of the population, no more than 5–10 percent, and that literacy, apart from very basic or "craftsman literacy," was far more common among the social elite. In addition, we noted that advanced skills in grammar and rhetoric were rarer still, comprising only a small percentage of those who were literate. A number of factors relating to access, relevance, social stratification, and the perception of limited good make it unlikely that anyone outside of the social elite would have gained such developed skills in these two subjects.

In chapter 2, we explored Luke's level of literacy by examining numerous features of his writing. Luke's advanced skills in both grammar and rhetoric are apparent in a host of stylistic and rhetorical devices his narrative displays and adapts to its own ends. His command of Greek and ability to adjust styles to suit speaker and occasion, to imitate classical style, or to create a form of Greek reminiscent of Israel's Scriptures, all reveal his mastery over the language. His use of multiple conventions common to ancient biographers and historians—some of which were common in rhetorical handbooks—shows his familiarity with his literary milieu and Greco-Roman rhetorical strategies. The creativity and artistry with which he integrates these devices into his sophisticated plotting and interweaving of themes indicate a writer of considerable talent. They also indicate that Luke was one who possessed the resources needed to cultivate his impressive literary skill.

The inevitable conclusion that emerges is that Luke was very likely among the social elite of his day. Other details from his writing could be marshaled to confirm this analysis. Luke reveals his familiarity with the formal proceedings involving the Roman elite (Acts 23:23–25:27), the reality of occasional enmity and alliance among the Roman hierarchy (Luke 23:6-12; Acts 25:13-27), and the types of appeals, pressures or motivations that compelled their decisions (Luke 23:23-25; Acts 5:17-42; 16:35-40; 19:23-24; 22:22-29; 23:12-22; 23:23–25:27).[1] In short, the sense that emerges from Luke's frequent portrayal of the Roman elite is that their world is one with which he is intimately acquainted. Of course, it is not *impossible* that Luke was a mere, scantily paid and little-honored tutor with genius-like ability and by some accident of fortune gained access to a wide berth of texts and the time to study them diligently, leading to the acquisition of impressive literary acumen that, after yet another accident of fortune granting him extended periods of leisure, he was able to employ in the crafting of his lengthy two-volume work. Indeed, history is filled with exceptions, and stranger things have happened. But such an exception is not nearly as probable as the likelihood that Luke was part of that upper echelon of society that had access to the literate education, literary texts, writing equipment, time, and resources he would have needed to develop the impressive repertoire of skills he came to possess and compose the writing that has been admired by so many. From this it also follows that Theophilus, whom Luke addresses with the honorary appellation of "most excellent" (Luke 1:3), was among Luke's fellow elite (see also Acts 23:26; 24:2; 26:7) and likely held an even higher social rank than the evangelist.

But what would it have meant, in Luke's day, to be part of the social elite, and how would his station in life compare to that of the rest of the populace in the Mediterranean world? In the introduction, I indicated that one's social location in antiquity is about more than simply what parties one was invited to. Most fundamentally, it is about access to power and resources and participation in the dominant myths that legitimize one's place in the order of things. The first section of this chapter attempts to shed some light on these matters. The second explores how Luke's membership among the elite might help us better appreciate the rhetorical edge of his writing.

The Social and Economic Structure of the Roman World

To begin, let us briefly explore what many anthropologists and social scientists have to say about the social and economic structure of the Roman world, including Roman Palestine. To get us started with this discussion, I offer the following diagram:

Diagram 3.1

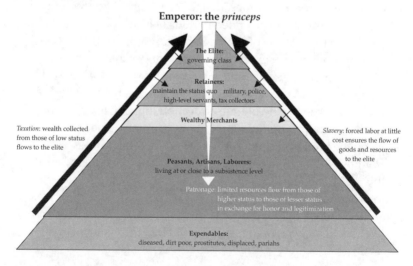

The hierarchical, social structure of the first-century Roman world was basically pyramidal. At its apex was the emperor, father of the empire, the first man (*princeps*), and its chief patron. To him was due the highest allegiance and honor. Directly beneath him were the elites, the ruling class, comprising no more than 2–5 percent of the population. This class was subdivided into several levels. The highest level was the senatorial rank, the most prestigious of all ranks whose membership was limited to several hundred families.[2] Below this was the equestrian rank, also requiring high birth, wealth, and moral excellence, but larger, numbering in the thousands. The decurion rank was next, comprised of those holding civil service jobs and administrative posts. In a continuum from the lower levels of this elite and ranging downward toward nonelite levels were retainers. This included "lower-level military officers, officials and bureaucrats such as clerks and bailiffs, personal retainers, household servants, scholars, legal experts, and lower-level lay aristocracy. These worked primarily in the service of the elite and served to mediate both governmental and religious functions to the lower class and to village areas."[3] Retainers also played a crucial role in the flow of goods and services from producers, primarily the lower classes, to the elite. While a small slice of the population enjoyed the good fortune of being wealthy merchants (some of whom managed to join the ranks of the elite), the vast majority of the population were peasants, including the urban nonelite (merchants, artisans, day laborers, and service workers), rural peasants (those owning and farming small land holdings, tenant farmers, day laborers), and village artisans and service workers. Beneath them were those who were viewed by most as outcasts: the dirt poor, diseased or severely handicapped, prostitutes, displaced, and other social pariahs.

One of the key features of Roman society the diagram seeks to convey is its economic "circulatory system." The lower class produced nearly all of the goods and services of the empire but retained very little of that wealth for themselves. Aggressive taxation, an elite-controlled market system that nickeled-and-dimed the underclass through rents and tariffs and underpaid them for their produce and/or labor, lending policies that routinely resulted in the foreclosure of peasant land holdings, and institutionalized slavery all ensured the flow of wealth and resources from the underclass to the elite, as depicted by the large and small black arrows on the diagram. The result of this hierarchical economy was that 2–5 percent of the population controlled about 85 percent of the empire's resources, leaving 95–98 percent of the population the difficult task of getting by with the remaining 15 percent. While conditions undoubtedly varied among the peasant class, and to a large extent were dependent on the state of the most recent harvest, many lived at or below a subsistence level.

Richard Rohrbaugh offers the following summary of how Roman economy and social hierarchy would have been manifested in Palestine:

> The urban elite made up about 2 percent of the total population. At its upper levels, the urban elite included the highest ranking military officers, ranking priestly families, and the Herodians and other ranking aristocratic families. They lived in the heavily fortified central areas of the cities . . . socially isolated from the rest of society. . . . The literacy rate among them was high, in some areas, even among women, and along with their retainers they maintained control of writing, coinage, taxation, and the military and judicial systems. Their control was powerfully legitimated by the religious and educational bureaucracy, which typically became the keepers of the so-called Great Tradition (the "official" version of the religious tradition, which only the elite could afford to practice, contrasted with the so-called Little Tradition, common among the lower classes). . . .
>
> The wealth of the elite was based primarily on land ownership and taxation, which effectively drained the resources of the rural areas. The "resdistributive" economic system, as it is called in economic anthropology, served to expropriate peasant surplus and redistribute it among those in control.[4]

There was, however, a form of redistribution in which resources did flow from those of higher to lower status. This system was called "patronage," consisting of a relationship between a patron and clients. Returning to the diagram, note the white arrow that descends from the emperor downward. The emperor functioned as the chief patron for the entire empire, as he sanctioned the distribution of wealth to its various members. In turn, the elite would also serve as patrons to elites of lesser status and perhaps even to members of the lower class, and this would continue down the social scale. What patrons would offer clients varied: financial and/or legal assistance during times of crisis, protection from enemies, food, gifts, mentoring, appointments to an official post, and ascribed honor, among other favors or forms of assistance. In return, the patron could expect to receive honor, information, and political support from clients.[5] Often, the relationship and exchanges between patron and client were face-to-face; at times favors and requests were mediated through an intermediary, or "broker." What the patron-client system amounted to was—to use a modern analogy—a rather meager form of trickle-down economics. While it often allowed for the dispersal of resources to those who needed them, the system was of equal if not greater value for the patrons themselves and actually served to maintain the imbalance of power. As K. C. Hanson and Douglas E. Oakman explain:

> Because of the hierarchical structure of power in the ancient world and the huge gap between "power elites" and the rest of the population, patronage functioned as the means by which elites could increase honor and status, acquire and hold office, achieve power and influence, and increase wealth. Patronage facilitated the maintenance of power differentials and control by those with power (patrons), exchanging their exercise of it on behalf of others (clients) in return for their client's support, honor, information and loyalty. In other words, it kept the social hierarchy intact. By acting in this way, networks of clients were developed.[6]

As the downward arrow indicates in the diagram, the dispersal of wealth generally lessened the further patronage went down the social scale. Through patronage, the greatest resources were disbursed to those already at or near the level of elite. For peasants, the resources received through patronage could be of great assistance but did not fundamentally alter their social and economic station. To put it differently, patronage among the upper classes was about favors, networking, and advancement. Patronage for the peasantry was about gaining resources that eased in varying degrees their struggle to stay out of debt (and thus avoid jail and/or slavery) and even to survive.

Elite Living

Access to Resources

If you were to visit the first-century Mediterranean world, or any other of the countless civilizations with steep social stratification, what would be immediately obvious about the elite is their access to relatively abundant material resources. The elite owned elaborately decorated and (relatively) spacious homes, some with large courtyards bordering manicured gardens. They ate from the choicest produce of the land, regularly feasted on meat, consumed the cleanest water, and sipped the best wine. They wore the finest linens and rode the swiftest horses. The same economic forces that gave the elite access to wealth also gave them access to cheap labor. The elite possessed or hired other persons—slaves and tenant laborers—who were obligated to perform a wide range of services at their bidding. The elite did not clean their spacious homes, raise their own crops or cattle, prepare their own meals, tend to their own horses, wash their own clothes, haul their own trash, fill their own baths, or empty their own pots. They paraded on streets they did not pave and sat in theatres, debated in halls, and worshiped at temples they did not build (though some may have paid for them as a gift to their city). In comparison to the vast majority of the population, the elite lived a life of privilege, even luxury. While some of the elite may have led busy lives overseeing their estates, managing their business affairs, and enhancing their social contacts, they likely had far more time for pursuing leisure activity and intellectual interests.

To be sure, the elite were not removed from the vicissitudes of an agonist (competitive) society (see below). They likely encountered repeated challenges to their honor. A coup or abrupt change of leadership could threaten their privileged station, and even their lives, if they were deemed irredeemably loyal to the overthrown regime. But much more so than the majority, the elite avoided deficiencies and situations that dramatically shortened life expectancy. Their access to regular nutrition, superior shelter, rudimentary healthcare and hygiene, and clean(er) water, their avoidance of hard, manual labor, and the protection of cities made it far more likely for them to live into what we call "middle age" than the rest of society.

> Obviously disease and high death rates were not evenly spread across all elements of the population but rather fell disproportionately upon the lower classes of both city and village. For most lower-class people who did make it to adulthood, their health would have been atrocious. By age thirty, the majority suffered from internal parasites, rotting teeth, and bad eyesight. Most had lived with the debilitating results of protein deficiency since childhood. Parasites were especially prevalent, being carried to humans by sheep, goats, and dogs. Fifty percent of the hair combs from Qumran, Masada, and Murabbat were infected with lice and lice eggs, probably reflecting conditions elsewhere (Zias, 1991, 148). If infant mortality rates, the age structure of the population, and pathological evidence from skeletal remains can be taken as indicators, malnutrition was a constant threat as well (Fiensy, 1991, 98).[7]

In sharp contrast to the relative well-being of the elite, the life expectancy of the urban peasantry was in the low twenties, and the rural peasantry in the low thirties. Infant mortality rates were about 30 percent, and over half of all peasants living past age one would fail to make it past age sixteen.[8] In contrast, the bodies and psyches of the elite avoided the physical trauma and level of anxiety that must have chronically plagued the peasantry. Many of the underclass were struggling to survive, their days filled with worry about the next harvest; the next tax, tribute, rent, or loan payment; and often the next meal.

Elevated Social Status and Sense of Worth

Most among the elite would have also possessed a view of themselves, others, and the world that differed sharply from the rest of the population. By virtue of their birth, kinship group (actual or "fictive"[9]), and place in society, by virtue of their ascribed and acquired honor, the elite saw themselves and their fellow elite as superior members of humanity. They embraced a worldview which claimed for them a pedigree, an elevated sense of morality, and even a divine mandate, all of which established them as the select few whose worth and potential for good was far greater than those outside their rank. These perceptions of worth and mandate legitimated, in their eyes, their near exclusive access to and control of power and wealth. As Bruce Malina comments:

> The roles, statuses, entitlements, and obligations of the political system were available to properly pedigreed persons from only the "best" families and were hence tied up with the kinship system. The political unit was likewise an economic and religious one: the ancient Mediterranean knew political economy and political religion (at the political level, there was no economy or religion separate from politics). Political concerns for effective collective action on behalf of the in-group were replicated in the application of force on out-groups, largely in the interest of fundamental domestic economic concerns: acquisition of more land, labor, animals, and the like. Political religion, in turn, employed the roles, values, and goals of politics in the articula-

tion and expression of religion: religious functionaries were
political personages; focus was on the deity(ies) as source
of power and might, expected to provide order, well being,
and prosperity for the body politic and its power wielders
(elites) to the benefit of subjects.[10]

In other words, the elite made the laws, and rightly so, for they
were the educated and virtuous. They established economic
policy, for they knew what was best for the empire as a whole.
They spoke for the gods and goddesses, for they had the training
and purity to access the divine mysteries and be the faithful
guardians of sacred tradition. They ruled the empire, for their
station was sanctioned by the emperor, who was in turn sanctioned by heaven. Throughout the Roman Empire, including
Roman Palestine, social status meant access to the power that
ran and shaped society. Participation in that system as a member
of the controlling class was an enactment of the fundamental
doctrine that social, economic, and religious power was the
divinely mandated vocation of the elite.

Participation in an Agonistic Culture

As discussed in chapter 1, much of ancient society revolved
around the increase and loss of honor. The Greco-Roman world,
especially among the elite and among those wanting to achieve
this social level, was highly competitive. Social jockeying to gain
closer proximity to cherished patrons, generous benefaction in
the form of monuments or public structures, political advancement, challenge and riposte exchanges, or the amassing and
display of wealth—all such activities took place within an agonistic context in which the goal was to outdo one another in the
acquisition of honor. In a society shaped by the perception of
"limited good," there was only so much honor to go around,
and the increased social worth of another or another's family,
especially a rival, meant another's decrease.

Acquiescence to the Roman Power Structure
among the Elite of Israel

For the Israelite elite during the first century in Palestine, consisting of those families well aligned with the Herodians, other Roman officials, and the families of leading priests, acquiescence to—if not acceptance of—Roman rule was necessary if they were to maintain their privileged station. In practice if not in spirit, these Israelites signed on to the apparent truth that Caesar ruled the world and participated in the hierarchical socio-economic structure that ensured their abundance at the expense of the many. Josephus, a contemporary of Luke, stands as one visible example of such acquiescence. Himself an Israelite, his transformation from an Israelite officer leading the fight against Rome during the Judean Revolt (67–70 CE) to a chronicler of Israelite history criticizing his fellow revolutionaries, and in turn receiving the generous patronage of Roman leaders, illustrates the malleable allegiance of Israelites among the elite. From our vantage point in history, it would be easy for us to pass judgment on the Israelite aristocracy of the first century in Palestine. But few of us have ever faced the stark choice they had to make. Acquiesce to Rome and their appointed underlings, the Herodians among others, and allow yourself and your family to maintain the connections and status enabling them to live well. Resist, and either break your ties with your family or take them down with you. The life of the underclass, as we have seen, wasn't pretty but rather was nasty, brutish, and short. For many, it was likely an easy decision to do all one could to avoid it. Undoubtedly for others, it was a difficult decision. But when the well-being, if not survival, of yourself and your family was on the line, well, what choice did you have? While numerous elements of Israelite sacred tradition speak against such collusion with foreign powers and the widespread neglect of the "alien, orphan and widow," several of the Israelite heroes of old (e.g., Joseph, David, Ezra, Nehemiah, and Daniel) found a way to serve both Yahweh and Gentile lords as members of the elite.

Perhaps these figures from their sacred story provided many of the Israelite elite a precedent that they saw as legitimizing their own collusion with foreign rule.

Luke the Elite Evangelist

Luke's social location, his membership among the elite of Palestinian society, can, I believe, help us better appreciate the reasons for which, and the ends to which, he wrote his two-volume work. Over the last century, the purposes of Luke-Acts have been variously understood, though in recent years scholars have begun to home in on a narrower constellation of interests. A once popular view still held by some readers is that Luke wanted to demonstrate to Roman leaders that Christianity was politically and socially benign, posing no threat to the current world order, and that it should be regarded as another sect of an accommodating Judaism.[11] The supposed motivation behind Luke's portrayal was to stop the occasional persecution of Christians by Roman officials or to secure Paul's release from Roman custody. On several levels, this assessment of Luke's purpose fits well with his social location. As a member of the elite with advanced literary skills, Luke would be well equipped to shape a narrative that not only conformed to Greco-Roman conventions but also effectively spoke to his audience. He would know the right things to have Jesus, Paul, and other leading characters say to demonstrate the harmless nature of the Christian movement. In addition, Luke himself would have a vested interest in such an agenda. Not only his well-being, but also his own status as a member of the elite, as a confessed Christian, was likely in jeopardy. Luke could have found a way to reconcile his Christian faith with his privileged station in society, and he was now calling on his fellow elite and Roman authorities to accept this civilized form of the Jesus movement. Perhaps this also clarifies the role of the "most excellent" Theophilus to whom the work is dedicated. His patronage may not be that of commissioning and funding the writing of the work but of potentially serving as an advocate for Luke and the Christian movement among the elite. Ben Witherington offers an account of Luke's purpose that coheres with the general contours of this view:

> Luke was concerned that all sorts of people, including some of the social elite like Theophilus, be able to embrace this new faith as one with a long and rich heritage, and as a religion that could exist peacefully within the Roman Empire. He wanted to make evident that the faith was not only for the least and the lost, but also for the most, first and found.[12]

The problem with this assessment of Luke's purpose is that it is difficult to reconcile with the dominant pulses of Luke's narrative. In fact, most recent commentaries on Luke and Acts find his main emphases falling elsewhere.[13] Taking Luke's preface at face value (Luke 1:1-4), most conclude that the evangelist meant his two-volume work as a source of assurance and instruction on "the matters fulfilled among us" (1:1) for either recent Hellenized (Greek and/or Israelite) converts to the Jesus movement or those on its fringes (possibly "God fearers"—Gentiles attracted to Israelite faith). Many also identify the rejection of Jesus by most of Israel as a concern Luke meant to address, emphasizing in response the rootedness of early Christianity in Israelite tradition. A few relatively recent studies have gone so far as to claim that rather than presenting "the Way" as politically and socially benign, Luke portrays the advent of God's reign in Jesus as that which does nothing less than undermine society as shaped by the social elite and "turn the world upside down" (Acts 17:6).[14] I believe that this is indeed one of the primary aims of Luke's narrative. Consider, for instance, how Mary's celebration of Jesus' awaited arrival must have sounded to Luke's fellow elite (Luke 1:46-55).

And Mary said,
"My soul magnifies the Lord,
    and my spirit rejoices in God my Savior,

for he has looked with favor on the lowliness of his servant.
  Surely, from now on all generations will call me blessed;
for the Mighty One has done great things for me,
  and holy is his name.
His mercy is for those who fear him
  from generation to generation.
He has shown strength with his arm;
  he has scattered the proud in the thoughts of their hearts.
He has brought down the powerful from their thrones,
  and lifted up the lowly;
he has filled the hungry with good things,
  and sent the rich away empty.
He has helped his servant Israel,
  in remembrance of his mercy,
according to the promise he made to our ancestors,
  to Abraham and to his descendants forever."

Some Christian readers, especially within North America, have tended to spiritualize and "de-economize" the references to the poor and rich in Mary's song and to the dramatic reversal of fortune that will characterize life in God's kingdom. The "poor" has been understood as a metaphor for the humble and contrite; the "hungry" are those who hunger for God. Accordingly, the "rich," "proud," and "powerful" are those who have turned away from God and spurned God's ways. There are, however, two telling factors challenging the notion that Luke meant to convey such a purely spiritualized understanding of these verses.

First, Luke's historical setting makes such a reading extremely unlikely. Within our North American context, it is common for people of faith to separate matters of religion from politics and economics. One of the consequences of this cultural trait is that North American Christians have for decades now embraced forms of interpretation that bypass many of the political and economic dimensions of the biblical texts, seeking from them primarily "spiritual" truths that in turn nurture a politically and economically benign spirituality. But such was not the case in Luke's day, and Luke's readers would not have thought of making such distinctions or avoiding such connections; it would not have even dawned on them to do so. For them, politics, economics, and faith were not segregated but inextricably intertwined. To them "rich" and "powerful" meant the elite, and "poor" and "hungry" meant peasants and other members of the underclass, even when they appeared in "religious" texts.[15]

Second, if Mary's announcement of socioeconomic reversal as a marker of God's coming kingdom were an isolated one, then it would be easier to consider that Luke meant it in a symbolic sense—or simply used the hymn for the sake of characterization—and thus easier to downplay its significance within Luke's conception of God's salvation. But so pervasive throughout Luke-Acts is this theme of social and economic reversal as a consequence of God's visitation in Jesus, and cast as a reversal that is to begin in the present, that a purely symbolic reading of Mary's hymn within the broader context of Luke-Acts is simply not viable.

Turning the World Upside Down

What I offer below is a brief listing of the various ways in which the theme of social and economic reversal is manifested in Luke-Acts, including, and overwhelmingly so, in material that is unique to Luke. Taken together, these frequent manifestations of the theme demonstrate Luke's interest in challenging elite privilege, values, and perspectives on the world.

1) Mary, an unwed mother who bears the Messiah of Israel, and the shepherds who in Luke 2 become the "first evangelists" of God's good news themselves reflect the elevation of the lowly that Mary announces in Luke 1.

2) In his summation of John's preaching, Luke alone records John's call for the sharing of clothing and food and for tax collectors and soldiers to refrain from extortion (3:10-14).

3) Luke alone has Jesus cite the Isaian oracles announcing the deliverance of the poor, the release of captives and the oppressed, and the year of jubilee (which includes the return of ancestral lands seized by the elite) as a summation of his ministry (4:16-19).

4) Luke's version of the sermon on the plain much more directly presents the reversal arriving with God's kingdom in socioeconomic terms (6:20-26; see also 14:7-14; compare to Matthew's version of the beatitudes in Matt 5:1-12). As the sermon continues, Jesus also instructs his followers to leave behind the patronage system and to give without calculation (6:27-36), thereby becoming "children of the Most High; for he is kind to the ungrateful and the wicked" (v. 35).

5) In his account of the widow's son at Nain (7:11-17), Luke mentions that the dead man "was his mother's only son, and she was a widow," thus underscoring the precarious economic situation of the woman who now lacks a male provider (v. 12).

6) Jesus elevates a "sinful" woman as a model of faithfulness, while Simeon the Pharisee is shown to be one of little love of God and others (7:36-50). See also the parable of the tax collector and Pharisee in Luke 18:9-14.

7) In his account of the Gerasene demoniac (8:26-39), Luke emphasizes the marginalization of the one who has been possessed. Luke identifies him as "a man of the city" and elaborates on his present state in relationship to his community: "For a long time he had worn no clothes, and did not live in a house but in the tombs" (v. 27). Shortly thereafter we are told that his community had tried to control his demonic outbursts by keeping him shackled and under guard, but to no avail. The man would break the bonds and be driven by the demon into the wilds (v. 29). There he was left alone to a desperate existence. The man is completely separated, culturally, socially, and geographically, from his

own people. Yet even to one such as this, God's gift of salvation is freely given. The man's subsequent desire to remain with Jesus and follow him stands in sharp contrast to the reaction of the civilized "city folk" to the dramatic display of Jesus' power. They "were afraid" when they saw the man healed (v. 35) and "seized with great fear" (v. 37) when told of the swine. Not so subtly, their response mirrors that of the demons who had possessed the man. They too react to the manifestation of God's presence and power in Jesus with great fear and can't wait to be rid of him.

8) The feeding story serves as an object lesson of what life will be like in the kingdom of God, where no one is hungry (9:10-17).

9) Jesus' teachings on discipleship call followers to sacrifice and forsake the ways of the world (9:23-27; 9:57-58), to put service to the kingdom above family honor and loyalty (9:59-62; 12:49-53; 14:25-33) and attempts to elevate their own honor (10:7; 11:43), and to radically recast their understanding of greatness (9:46-48).

10) Jesus offers several parables and teachings warning against the pursuit of wealth and status that are unique to or heavily redacted by Luke: the rich fool (12:13-21), the great dinner (14:15-24; see also 14:25-33), the dishonest manager (16:1-13), and the rich man and Lazarus (16:19-31). See also the story of Zacchaeus, the tax collector, who after dining with Jesus gives half of his possessions to the poor and repents of defrauding them. In response, Jesus announces that Zacchaeus' actions signify the presence of God's salvation (19:1-10). Jesus also calls his disciples to take stock of what their commitment to him and the kingdom will entail, using the parables of one who builds a tower and a king who goes out to war to illustrate the importance of counting the cost (14:25-32). But then Jesus describes that cost in very personal, economic terms: "So therefore, none of you can become my disciple if you do not give up all your possessions" (14:33).

11) Luke-Acts presents to us a striking contrast between the economy and fate of the temple verses the economy of the household and its place in the arrival of God's new age.[16] For Luke, the temple system—its administration, distribution of resources, and promotion of socioeconomic status— epitomizes the world order that the kingdom of God would overthrow. As John Elliot summarizes,

> The temple, once a holy house of prayer had become a "den of thieves" (Luke 19:46). The guardians of the temple law, purity, and power had become preoccupied with status and class determination (Luke 11:43, 52; 15:2; 16:5; 18:11). They imposed heavy burdens (Luke 11:46), ignored the needy (Luke 10:29-37), neglected justice and the love of God (Luke 11:42), were full of extortion and wickedness (Luke 11:39), and devoured widows' houses (Luke 20:7). . . . Precisely because it had failed in the *redistribution* not only of material resources but also justice, mercy, and peace, the entire system and its chief symbol, the temple, was destined by God for destruction (Luke 11:34-35; 19:41-44; 21:5-6, 20-24).[17]

In marked contrast, the communities of Jesus' followers in the gospels and that of early believers in Acts display communal life marked by the reciprocities of kinship, friendship, and social relations characterized by intimacy and inclusivity. Moreover, "resources were not directed under compulsion to a distant center and redistributed according to the interests of those in power, but were shared directly according to availability and need (Luke 6:3-36; 11:5-13; 12:33; 15:3-32; 18:22; 19:1-10; Acts 2:44-47; 5:32-37; 6:1-6)."[18] To us, the household churches and their economy may seem rather quaint, even naïve, but they constitute a striking rejection of the Roman and Judean economies, in which distribution of resources was based on social location and power, not need. The practices of the early believers also set aside the engrained cultural notion of limited good.

12) Luke implicates not only the Israelite elite in Jesus' death but also Herod and Pilate (Acts 4:27). He further reports that it was Herod who "laid violent hands upon some who belonged to the church," including James and Peter (12:1-3). Overall, Herod Agrippa is portrayed by Luke as ruthless and proud (12:1-23). Governor Felix does not fare much better. He appears as fearful, immoral, and money hungry (24:24-27). Through these characterizations, Luke unveils the depravities of the elite, in contrast to the virtue of believers, many of whom society tends to hold without esteem.

13) The ministry of the disciples in Acts is repeatedly depicted as bringing hope, comfort, and healing to the poor and diseased, echoing Jesus' own ministry to the marginalized in the gospel (3:1-10; 5:12-16; 8:4-8; 9:36; 14:8-9; 19:12).

14) Two major conflicts in response to Paul's ministry are instigated by the threat his ministry poses for economic gain. Paul casts a spirit of divination out of a slave girl in Philippi, depriving her owners of easy income, leading to the beating and arrest of Paul and his companions (16:16-24). The riot in Ephesus was started by silversmiths who rightly perceived that Paul's teaching against idolatry would be bad for business (19:23-41).

15) Luke repeatedly makes it clear that the authority to proclaim the mysteries of God resides not in a select few, but in an ever-expanding group of ministers and eyewitnesses. While the ministry of the Twelve receives focused attention, the pattern presented in both the gospel and Acts is that the ministry and authority of witness is to be taken up by many others as well. Luke alone among the evangelists pairs and follows the sending out of the Twelve (Luke 9) with the sending out of the seventy (Luke 10), the latter receiving the same commission and authority as the Twelve. Similarly, in Acts the ministry of the Twelve is soon overshadowed

by those outside the original apostolic circle, including Stephen, Philip, and a formerly deadly enemy of the church, Saul. Unlike his fellow elite, Luke does not see the mysteries of heaven as confined to the learned. After the seventy return and share their experiences with Jesus, Jesus exclaims

> I thank you, Father, Lord of heaven and earth, because you have hidden these things from the wise and the intelligent and have revealed them to infants; yes, Father, for such was your gracious will. All things have been handed over to me by my Father; and no one knows who the Son is except the Father, or who the Father is except the Son and anyone to whom the Son chooses to reveal him. (10:21-22)

For Luke, the authority to disclose the mysteries of heaven resides in the call of God, and that call comes to folks across the social spectrum—to priests, women, shepherds, widows, fishermen, tax collectors, former demoniacs, Pharisees, and prostitutes, among others.

What we witness in Luke's narrative, as this cursory listing displays, is Luke's direct challenge to the world of the upper class. Note how the privilege and ideological commitments of the elite we discussed earlier are countered by Luke's shaping of his account. Resources are not to be zealously horded and enjoyed by a few. They are to be distributed according to need, not social location. The elite and learned are not the only, or the most reliable, guardians of sacred tradition. Rather, the good news that matters most for humankind is being announced by apostles who are "uneducated and ordinary men" (Acts 4:13) and given voice by an ever-expanding group of witnesses from across the social spectrum. Believers are called not to participate in the agonistic quest for honor or the system of patronage that merely perpetuates the status quo, but to redefine their understanding of greatness as service and humility and to lend without the expectation of reciprocity.

Serving Another Lord

Along with presenting the socioeconomic oppression of the Roman Empire as an evil God's kingdom shall overthrow, Luke also makes it clear near the start of his narrative that there is only one Lord whom Christians are to regard as the savior of humankind and offer their unconditioned allegiance. Consider Luke's account of Jesus' birth followed by the angelic announcement proclaiming him "Savior" and "Messiah Lord" (Luke 2:1-14).

> In those days a decree went out from Emperor Augustus that all the world should be registered. This was the first registration and was taken while Quirinius was governor of Syria. All went to their own towns to be registered. Joseph also went from the town of Nazareth in Galilee to Judea, to the city of David called Bethlehem, because he was descended from the house and family of David. He went to be registered with Mary, to whom he was engaged and who was expecting a child. While they were there, the time came for her to deliver her child. And she gave birth to her firstborn son and wrapped him in bands of cloth, and laid him in a manger, because there was no place for them in the inn.
>
> In that region there were shepherds living in the fields, keeping watch over their flock by night. Then an angel of the Lord stood before them, and the glory of the Lord shone around them, and they were terrified. But the angel said to them, "Do not be afraid; for see—I am bringing you good news of great joy for all the people: to you is born this day in the city of David a Savior, who is the Messiah, the Lord. This will be a sign for you: you will find a child wrapped in bands of cloth and lying in a manger." And suddenly there was with the angel a multitude of the heavenly host, praising God and saying,
>
> > "Glory to God in the highest heaven,
> >   and on earth peace among those whom he favors!"

Throughout the preceding episodes of the infancy narrative, including Mary's hymn, Luke employs reversal and paradox to help his readers appreciate that the kingdom inaugurated in the conceptions and births of John and Jesus is one that will turn the tables on the current world order. The crescendo in Luke's portrayal of this "upside-down" world in the infancy narrative takes place here in the story of Jesus' birth. With a concentration of dramatic artistry that is remarkable even for Luke, the evangelist smoothly but not so subtly invites readers to discern, embrace, and praise the one who is truly Lord and to join those who praise and bear witness to the world's one true Savior.

Yet as the passage opens, it is the one known to the Mediterranean world and beyond as Lord who speaks and moves "all the world" to action (2:1). Caesar Augustus, the Roman emperor and father of the empire, orders a census to be taken and his underlings, such as Quirinius, governor of Syria, make it happen. Caesar wants to take stock of his subjects and possessions, the objects of his rule and sources of revenue. His word is spoken, and the world has no choice but to comply with this "penetrating symbol of Roman overlordship." [19] And so, "all went to their own towns to be registered" (v. 3). The father of Jesus is no exception: "Joseph also went from the town of Nazareth in Galilee to Judea, to the city of David called Bethlehem" (v. 4). Caesar's command rules the cosmos, or so it seems.

Scholars have long noted and debated a serious problem with Luke's chronology here. As many point out, reliable historical sources place the reign of Quirinius and the census undertaken while he was governor several years later in 6 CE. [20] We will not engage this debate here, but note that is common for scholars to view the census as a device employed by the evangelist to get Mary and Joseph to Bethlehem. In their view, Luke may be fudging a bit with the dating or may simply be mistaken, but he needs to place Jesus' birth in Bethlehem in order to cohere with early Christian tradition and fulfill Micah 5:2-4, which identifies this little Judean village as the birthplace of the Messiah (see Matt 2:1-6 and Matthew's citation of Micah 5:2-4 [5:1-4 in the HB]).

Luke's interest in Bethlehem for these reasons seems likely, but the census serves other interests as well. If Luke, along with Matthew, understands Jesus' birth in Bethlehem as the divinely ordained fulfillment of Micah's prophecy, then notice how the mighty rule of Caesar is already being undercut in the opening verses of Luke's account. Ironically and unknowingly, Caesar Augustus, the world's venerated sovereign, puts into motion events that lead to the fulfillment of God's will for Israel and all the world.[21] For, as the reader's attention is shifted from Caesar to Joseph, Mary, and the child they will bear, the mention of the city, house, and lineage of David reminds the reader of Jesus' messianic identity and once again grounds him in the soil of Judaism (v. 4). Caesar rules the world, including Palestine, but Israel's Messiah, who will deliver Israel from its enemies, is about to be born (cf. 1:71, 74). And Caesar helps to bring it all to pass, unknowingly pushing the unborn Messiah to Bethlehem, that he might be born just as God "spoke through the mouth of his holy prophets from of old" (1:70).

In her song of praise, Mary announced that the coming of her child would result in the bringing down of the powerful from their thrones and the lifting up of the lowly (1:52). But even this warning leaves the reader unprepared for Luke's description of Jesus' birth and humble state of his first resting place. In simple, unadorned prose, we are told that Jesus is born, wrapped in bands of cloth, and laid in a feedbox "because there was no place for them in the inn" (2:7). It can't get much lowlier than this. The *kataluma*, the hostel-like shelter or room set aside for travelers adjoining a house, is full.[22] None move aside so that the very pregnant and eventually laboring Mary can give birth in the security of even these very sparse quarters. So the young couple nestles in among the sheep, goats, and chickens, delivers their child, and employs a manger for a crib. It may sound romantically rustic to us, but Luke's readers are confronted with an image of Israel's Messiah that could not be more incongruous with the pomp and might of Emperor Augustus on his throne, commanding the world at will. The repeated references to the bands of cloth and manger as the "sign" that identifies Jesus (2:12, 16-17) keep these lowly elements in view even as he is exalted by the heavenly host and found by the shepherds.

As the scene shifts from stable to darkened field, we once again encounter a setting far removed from Caesar's seat in Rome: shepherds tending their flocks by night. This is another element of the story that modern readers have long romanticized. But the lowliness of the shepherds and the locale of their labor would have held social and political overtones for Luke's readers. Recall our earlier discussion of Roman society and economy. Shepherds, as well as all agricultural workers, were among the large peasant class whose economic servitude fueled the economy of empire and hegemony of Roman rule. Their economic exploitation was maintained by their lack of social and political standing. As Joel B. Green explains,

> Shepherds in an agrarian society may have small landholdings, but these would be inadequate to meet the demands of their own families, the needs of their own agricultural pursuits, and the burden of taxation. As a result, they may hire themselves out to work for wages. There were, then, peasants, located toward the bottom of the scale of power and privilege. That they are here cast in this dress is unmistakable, for the same contrast introduced in Mary's song—the enthroned versus the lowly (1:52)—is represented here: Augustus the Emperor and Quirinius on the one hand (2:1-2), the shepherds on the other.[23]

To claim that the birth of this child of Israel and his manifestation in this agrarian setting so far removed from the center of Roman rule poses any sort of meaningful challenge to Caesar would, by nearly all sane accounts of the time, be simply laughable. But this is just the announcement that explodes into the darkened night as an angelic host appears and the very glory of God engulfs the shepherds.[24] That Luke intended his readers to hear this birth announcement as an implied, but quite apparent, repudiation of Caesar's reign is indicated by the fact that many of the very same things celebrated about Caesar and his birth are now attributed to this infant lying in a feedbox. In their decision to honor Augustus by beginning the new year on his birthday, the Roman provincial assembly announced,

> Whereas the providence which divinely ordered our lives created with zeal and munificence the most perfect good for our lives by producing Augustus . . . for the *benefaction of mankind*, sending us a *savior* who put an end to war . . . and whereas the *birthday* of the god marked *for the world* the beginning of *good tidings* through his coming.[25]

The parallels to the angel's announcement in 2:10-11 are apparent:

> Do not be afraid; for see—I am bringing you *good news* of great joy for *all the people*: to you is *born this day* in the city of David a *Savior*, who is the Messiah Lord. (my translation and emphasis)

As Richard Horsley comments:

> Any reader or hearer of this story in the Hellenistic-Roman world, particularly in Palestine, would have understood here a direct opposition between Caesar, the savior who had supposedly brought peace, and the child proclaimed as the savior, whose birth means peace. Luke clearly understands Jesus to be in direct confrontation with the emperor, for here finally is the birth of the messiah in the city of David that the stories and particularly the songs in Luke 1 are proclaiming and eagerly anticipating.[26]

Beyond these allusions to the Roman celebration of Augustus, there were other claims of Roman lordship that would have been scorched upon the hearts of those sympathetic to traditional Israelite hopes. In the aftermath of the Judean revolt, Roman supporters added insult to tragedy by claiming that Vespasian or his son, Titus—the Roman heroes in the defeat of Jerusalem who were later crowned emperor—were the ones that fulfilled the Israelite messianic prophecies of old! The Israelite general turned historian, Josephus, who entered into the service of Titus after the revolt, proclaimed:

> But what more than all else incited them [the Jews] to war was an ambiguous oracle, likewise found in their sacred scriptures, to the effect that at that time one from their own country would become ruler of the world. This they understood to mean someone from their own race, and many of their wise men went astray in their interpretation of it. The oracle, however, in reality signified the sovereignty of Vespasian, who was proclaimed Emperor on Jewish soil.[27]

Likewise, the Roman historian Tacitus announced:

> Few [Jews] interpreted these omens [portending the fall of Jerusalem] as fearful; the majority firmly believed that their ancient priestly writings contained a prophecy that this was the very time when the East should grow strong and that men starting from Judea should possess the world. This mysterious prophecy had in reality pointed to Vespasian and Titus, but the common people, as is the way of human ambition, interpreted these great destinies in their own favor and could not be turned even by adversity.[28]

In not so subtle contrast to the prevailing Roman propaganda of the day, Luke has the angels present the bold counterclaim that Jesus, not Caesar, is Lord and Savior. They announce that it is the birth of this infant, resting in a feedbox, that is truly *euangelion* ("good news") for "all the people."[29] He, not the emperor, will be the one to bring peace to all those on whom God's favor rests. When one takes into account the way in which Luke converges the characters of Jesus and God throughout the infancy narrative (recall Luke's use of step-parallelism as discussed in chap. 2), including here with the titles "Savior" and "Lord," Luke's challenge dramatically relayed is this: the Israelite infant lying in a feedbox among sheep, goats, cattle, and fowl, drastically marginalizes the significance of Caesar and Rome itself, as he manifests the presence and power of God. For *his* birthday, not Caesar's, is truly good news for all of humankind. He, not Caesar, is Lord and Savior of the world. His reign, not Caesar's, will lead the heavens to erupt in praise of God (not the gods) and in the celebration of enduring peace: "Glory to God in the highest heaven, and on earth peace among those whom he favors" (vv. 13-14). This, Luke shows, is how God's plan for the redemption of Israel, and even all humanity, unfolds. In this peasant infant, God does nothing less than come into the world and turn it upside down.

Thus, already near the start of his narrative, Luke puts Theophilus and the rest of his audience on notice that what God does in Jesus significantly undermines all other claims to mastery over humankind. In doing so, he also provides the interpretive context for understanding the significance of the titles "Messiah" (*Christos*) and "Lord" (*kurios*) in the remainder of his narrative. *Jesus is the long-awaited King of Israel. His will shall prevail for God's people, Israel. And more than that, because Yahweh rules over all the world, his son Jesus, not Caesar, is Lord and Savior of all.* Consequently, as Luke continues to exalt Jesus as Messiah and Lord (e.g., Luke 4:41; 6:5; 7:6; 9:20, 54; 10:1, 17; 11:1; 13:15, 23, 35; 19:8, 34, 38; 20:42-44, 64; 23:2l; 24:26, 34; Acts 1:6, 24; 2:21, 26; 3:20; 4:25-26; 9:22; 16:31; 17:3; 18:5; 19:5; 26:23) he presents a clear challenge to the authority of Rome and all who seek to extend its rule.

Consider also the following passage from Acts, in which Luke draws on the enthronement hymn of Psalm 2. Concluding the story of Peter and John's arrest by "the priests, the captain of the temple, and the Sadducees" and their release from prison (4:1-22), Luke again makes it clear that all earthly dominion and power pales in comparison to that held by the "Sovereign Lord" and "his Messiah."

After they were released, they went to their friends and reported what the chief priests and the elders had said to them. When they heard it, they raised their voices together to God and said, "Sovereign Lord, who made the heaven and the earth, the sea, and everything in them, it is you who said by the Holy Spirit through our ancestor David, your servant:

'Why did the Gentiles rage,
    and the peoples imagine vain things?
The kings of the earth took their stand,
    and the rulers have gathered together
        against the Lord and against his Messiah.'

For in this city, in fact, both Herod and Pontius Pilate, with the Gentiles and the peoples of Israel, gathered together against your holy servant Jesus, whom you anointed, to do whatever your hand and your plan had predestined to take place. And now, Lord, look at their threats, and grant to your servants to speak your word with all boldness, while you stretch out your hand to heal, and signs and wonders are performed through the name of your holy servant Jesus." When they had prayed, the place in which they were gathered together was shaken; and they were all filled with the Holy Spirit and spoke the word of God with boldness. (4:23-31)

Luke may not be calling for armed revolt. But he is challenging his readers' allegiances, urging them to forsake the life carved out for them by "the kings of the earth" and to speak with all boldness about life in a new kingdom under a new king. The tide has turned, Luke announces. This new kingdom is already beginning to overtake the old. And having turned the reader's attention to Psalm 2, the implications seem clear: someday soon the foundations of Rome and all earthy claims to power—these God's Messiah "shall break . . . with a rod of iron, and dash . . . in pieces like a potter's vessel!" (Ps 2:8-9). Augustus, Titus, Vespasian, the Judean governors, and the Herods—their claims to sovereignty and beneficence are the source of divine derision and wrath (see Ps 2:4-5). God has set his king on high (Ps 2:6), and "there is salvation in no one else, for there is no other name under heaven given among mortals by which we must be saved" (Acts 4:12).

Reassessing Luke's Purposes

To argue that the aim of Luke's two volume work is to assure the Roman elite that Christianity poses no threat to the stability of the world that has served them so well, is, in my view, to completely misunderstand one of its fundamental aims. To the contrary, in order to gain a more complete and faithful understanding of the purposes of Luke-Acts, we need to attend carefully to its repeated calls for socio-economic reversal, the rhetorical edginess of the narrative, and Luke's own social location.

As an elite, Luke was well positioned, socially and educationally, to reach out to his peers. His impressive literary talent would have also served as a valuable asset, enabling him to cloak his bold rhetorical aims in the seductive ploy of storytelling. But what perhaps best equipped Luke as an evangelist to his fellow elite was that he was calling them to embark on a journey that he himself had already begun to tread. Luke had already made the remarkable, and countercultural, commitment to give up his status as an elite. He chose the distribution of resources "as any had need" over the system that had granted him and his family access to so much at the expense of so many. He set aside the pretentious claim that his worth and authority as an elite transcended that of most other persons inhabiting the world for a vision in which all people, especially the poor and marginalized, are called to take part in the bounty and stewardship of God's new age. Luke distanced himself from the daily pursuit of honor and replaced it with the call to take up daily the humiliation of the cross as he followed in the self-giving footsteps of Jesus, a crucified criminal of the state. Finally, Luke looked beyond the thrones of Caesar and his underlings and found another Lord and kingdom to which all his allegiance was due. Luke thus writes to his once-fellow elites, Theophilus among others, not to convince them that this ridiculous little sect poses no threat to the world that has given them so much. Instead, he calls them to join him in leaving behind the kingdom of Rome, with all of its privileges, trappings, and inequities, to seek another, radically different realm and to align themselves with another crowd and a much greater Lord.

CONCLUSION

So Who Was Luke?

In the introduction, I briefly reviewed the debate regarding the identity of the writer of Luke-Acts. There I indicated my openness to the traditional claim that the writer was "Luke, the beloved physician," the companion of Paul referenced in Colossians 4:14. I also found compelling the perspective that Luke himself was an Israelite, as suggested by several factors:

1) Luke's intimate knowledge of Israel's sacred tradition

2) the similarities between his work and the historical writings of Israel's Scriptures, including their respective uses of direct and indirect discourse, immersion in sacred tradition, widespread use of allusion, and their repeated contextualization of the events they depict within the larger history of God's relationship with Israel

3) the close verbal and conceptual parallels between Luke's writing and texts found at Qumran, indicating that Luke was also familiar with this more marginalized stream of Palestinian Israelite tradition, and perhaps even associated with Essenes

4) Luke's positive regard for matters of piety and purity in his gospel and reluctance to have Jesus or Paul downplay the abiding importance of dietary restrictions

What I offer in this concluding chapter is a brief portrait of the evangelist that builds on his social location, literary acumen, and these additional factors suggesting that he was a son of Israel. While the sketchy caricature I present is rooted in elements of Luke's identity for which I believe there is telling evidence, I offer it as a creative venture, recognizing that it takes us well beyond the realm of what can be assuredly demonstrated.

A Portrait of Luke

Luke was born into an elite family that was part of the Israelite aristocracy of Palestine or Syria. His familiarity with and internalization of Israel's sacred tradition suggest that his may have been a priestly family.[1] Though committed to its Israelite heritage, this family was also thoroughly Hellenized or becoming increasingly so. The family sought education for its sons that would enable them to be intellectually well-heeled and honored among both their fellow Israelite aristocracy and the Gentile elite of the region who were part of their associations. Thus, Luke became well studied in Israel's sacred tradition as well as Greek grammar, rhetoric, and literature. He may have eventually taken a particular interest in medicine, thus earning him the designation or nickname of "physician." His intellectual abilities in these fields were remarkable and very likely they positioned him well for advancement into the upper echelons of the Palestinian elite.

I suspect, given the turns that Luke's life would later take, that from an early time Luke was occasionally plagued by a nagging sense that something about his privileged life just wasn't quite right. Perhaps it was brought on by a reading from the eighth-century prophets Amos or Micah or the first part of Isaiah. Perhaps it was the occasional glimpses of peasant life on his family's estate, of the urban poor as he traveled around town, or of the life of servitude by his family's own slaves. Undoubtedly, the pressures for him to conform to the social mores of his station were compelling. Not only his honor but also his family's honor would have been elevated by any social advancement he could achieve. He was his family's son, and the greatest expectation placed on his shoulders was to do them proud. Even so, though repeatedly repressed and ignored, the nagging continued, and sometimes he may have indulged it long enough to wonder.

We cannot say for sure when Luke's break from his family and life among the elite began. Was it a gradual disillusionment, taking place over a period of months or even years? Had one of the radical, apocalyptic preachers among the Israelite peasantry (an Essene?) suddenly caught his attention and led him to flee his life of privilege in order to be counted among the faithful? Or was it the preaching of early Christians, perhaps even Paul himself, that had started Luke down a very different path? What does seem very likely is that Luke joined the Jesus movement by the early fifties, traveling for a time with the Apostle Paul. This alone would have entailed a significant departure from the life he once knew.

And yet, it is hard to know to what extent Luke had distanced himself from his family and social location after he became involved with Paul. Would his radical change of vocation have led to an intractable rift between himself and his family? Had Luke, at this point, cast aside all of his possessions to become a follower of Jesus? Between his travels with Paul and the writing of Luke-Acts some twenty to thirty years later, we can't be sure to what extent he maintained connections to his life of privilege.

It seems likely to me, however, that Luke's movement away from his participation in the life of an elite was a gradual one and probably wasn't close to complete until shortly before or after the writing Luke-Acts. Two factors suggest that this was the case. First, Luke's own work as a historian, and the mastery of Greco-Roman (including Israelite) literary convention his work displays, indicates that he must have possessed the resources needed to continue pursuing his literary craft in the years following his companionship with Paul. Despite his involvement in the countercultural Jesus movement, his own studying and writing continued and necessitated access to large amounts of time and large numbers of texts. As we saw in chapter 1, such work would be very unlikely for someone who was not among the elite. Second, Luke's address to Theophilus and his intent to challenge his fellow elite to abandon all for the sake of Christ reveal that Luke had maintained connections to persons belonging to this social class. His gospel, while challenging, is much more pastoral in tone than condemnatory. To be sure, the rhetoric of Luke and Acts is pointed and sharp, and any members of his elite audience, including Theophilus, among others, who dared to carefully attend to his two volumes would surely feel its sting. Yet Luke did not turn on his own, though many of his fellow elite—likely including his own family—may have felt this way. Rather, Luke was calling them to a new vision of relatedness to God and one another, one based not on social location or patronage, or one's proximity to Caesar or the Palestinian aristocracy, but one at home in the new kingdom Jesus had begun to fashion around them. Luke wanted his fellow elite who had just joined the Christian movement or were considering it to know what they were in for. He also hoped for them to catch a glimpse of just how full of blessing this new life in God's reign could be:

> Do not be afraid, little flock, for it is your Father's good pleasure to give you the kingdom. Sell your possessions, and give alms. Make purses for yourselves that do not wear out, an unfailing treasure in heaven, where no thief comes near and no moth destroys. For where your treasure is, there your heart will be also. (Luke 12:32-34)

Perhaps Luke took a lesson from Paul's missionary manual and became—or remained—that which his target audience needed him to be (see 1 Cor 9:20-21; cf. Acts 17:16-32). Perhaps he maintained his elite status for a time so that he could continue the literary work he felt God was calling him to do. Perhaps it was the shock of the Judean revolt and the resulting tragic loss of life and destruction that finally pushed Luke away from the ranks of the elite and their collusion with the Romans (contra Josephus!). Or perhaps he, like those to whom he wrote his gospel, struggled to finally let go of the privilege and allegiances his life as an elite granted him and his two-volume work was just as much for his sake as it was for theirs. In any case, his writing was a call for other elites to hear what it was that he heard Jesus saying to him and to join him on a journey that he himself had begun.

NOTES

Note to Introduction (pages 1–13)

1. Nearly all scholars of the gospel and Acts believe that both works were written by the same writer due to the overwhelming similarity of style and theological perspective, their address to a certain "Theophilus" in the prologue to each (see Luke 1:1-4 and Acts 1:1-5), and the fact that the prologue of Acts refers to the gospel, "the first book" (Acts 1:1-2). Many readers, including me, regard the gospel and Acts as a two-volume work, hence the common designation, "Luke-Acts."

2. For the following summary I am indebted to Joseph A. Fitzmyer, *The Gospel According to Luke I–IX*, AB 28 (New York: Doubleday, 1981), 34–41.

3. Cited by ibid., 38.

4. A recent proponent of this view is Jürgen Wehnert, *Die Wir-Passagen der Apostelgeschichte: Ein lukanisches Stilmittel aus jüdischer Tradition* (Göttingen: Vandenhoeck & Ruprecht, 1989). See also E. Haenchen, " 'We' in Acts and the Itinerary," in *The Bultmann School of Biblical Interpretation: New Directions?* JTC 1 (Tübingen: Mohr; New York: Harper, 1965), 59–68.

5. Vernon K. Robbins, "By Land and by Sea: The We Passages and Ancient Sea Voyages," in *Perspectives in Luke-Acts*, ed. C. H. Talbert (Edinburg: T & T Clark, 1978), 215–42.

6. See the critiques offered by Ben Witherington III, *Acts of the Apostles: A Social-Rhetorical Commentary* (Grand Rapids, MI: Eerdmans, 1998), 483; Joseph A. Fitzmyer, *The Acts of the Apostles*, AB 31 (New York: Doubleday, 1997), 100–103; Fitzmyer, *Luke the Theologian: Aspects of His Teaching* (Mahwah, NJ: Paulist, 1989), 16–23; C. K. Barrett, "Paul Shipwrecked," in *Scripture, Meaning and Method*, ed. B. P. Thompson (Hull: Hull University Press, 1987), 51–63.

7. Witherington, *Acts*, 483.

8. D. D. Schmidt, "Syntactical Style in the 'We'-Sections of Acts: How Lucan Is It?" in *SBL1989 Seminar Papers*, 300–308.

9. Fitzmyer, *Luke I–IX*, 48.

10. Ibid., 49.

11. Rick Strelan, *Luke the Priest: The Authority of the Author of the Third Gospel* (Burlington: Ashgate, 2008), 161.

12. Robert Brawley, *Luke-Acts and Jews: Conflict, Apology and Conciliation* (Atlanta: Scholars Press, 1987), 157, cited in Strelan, *Luke the Priest*, 162.

13. Throughout this work I will avoid using the terms "Jew" and "Jewish" to refer to those persons, groups, and beliefs connected to Israelite religious tradition. John H. Elliot, following others, has persuasively argued that the proper translation of the term *Ioudaios* is not "Jew" but rather "Judean" (see "Jesus the Israelite Was neither a 'Jew' nor a 'Christian': On Correcting Misleading Nomenclature," *JSHJ* 5 [2007]: 119–54). Elliot also points out that this term was typically used by Gentiles to refer to those connected with Israelite ethnicity and faith. The preferred and much more common self-designations employed by members of this ethnicity and faith tradition were "Israelites," or "children of Israel," though at times Israelite writers did refer to other Israelites as *Ioudaioi* when addressing Gentile audiences. For this reason, I will follow Elliot's suggestion to adopt the preferred terminology of Israelites in Luke's day when I refer to these persons and their tradition, employing the terms "Israel," "House of Israel," "Israelite(s)," and "children of Israel."

14. Brooke, "Luke-Acts and the Qumran Scrolls: The Case of the MMT," in *Luke's Literary Achievement*, JSNTSup 116 (Sheffield: Sheffield Academic Press, 1995), 77. On the parallels between Luke 1:32-35 and 4Q246, see Karl A. Kuhn, "The 'One like a Son of Man' Becomes the 'Son of God,'" *CBQ* 69 (2007): 22–42.

15. Strelan, *Luke the Priest*, 105.

Notes to Chapter 1 (pages 14–37)

1. William V. Harris, *Ancient Literacy* (Cambridge, MA: Harvard University Press, 1989).

2. Harris, *Ancient Literacy*, 11–12.

3. See ibid., 11–24, 327.

4. Ibid., 13.

5. Ibid., 272.

6. Ibid., 173.

7. Ibid., 276–82.

8. Ibid., 284.

9. For a helpful and representative response to Harris' work, see the essays collected in J. H. Humphrey, ed., *Literacy in the Roman World*, Journal of Roman Archaeology Supplementary Series 3 (Ann Arbor: University of Michigan, 1991). Writing over a decade later, Catherine Hezser (*Jewish Literacy in Roman Palestine*, Texts and Studies in Ancient Palestine 81 [Tübingen: Mohr-Siebeck, 2001], 26) says of Harris' work: "Harris' monograph must be considered a milestone in the historical approach to the subject. Hardly anyone has questioned his low estimate of the literacy rate in the ancient world."

10. H. Gregory Snyder, *Teachers and Texts in the Ancient World: Philosophers, Israelites and Christians*, Religion in the First Christian Centuries (New York: Routledge, 2000), 215.

11. Ibid., 164.

12. 4Q266 fr. 5 ii: "And anyone whose [speech] is too soft (?) or speaks with a staccato voice not dividing his words so that [his voice] may be heard, none of these shall read from the book of the law, lest he cause error in a capital matter." 1QS 7.1: "If he blasphemed—either by being terrified with affliction or because of any other reason, while he is reading the book or saying benedictions—he shall be excluded and never again return to the Council of the Community." Cited by Snyder, *Teachers and Texts*, 146.

13. Ibid., 164.

14. Martin Jaffee, *Torah in the Mouth: Writing and Oral Tradition in Palestinian Judaism, 200 BCE–400 CE* (New York: Oxford University Press, 2001), 15.

15. Ibid. Similarly, James L. Crenshaw (*Education in Ancient Israel: Across the Deadening Silence* [New York: Doubleday, 1998], 12) also concludes that literacy was uncommon in ancient Israel. Even in Philo's day, "only upper-class Israelites studied the encyclia."

16. See Hezser, *Jewish Literacy*, 496–504.

17. Teresa Morgan, *Literate Education in the Hellenistic and Roman Worlds*, Cambridge Classical Studies (Cambridge: Cambridge University Press, 1998).

18. Morgan (ibid., 73): "I am pessimistic about levels of literacy in provincial cities—and indeed, in metropolitan cities—in general. The cultured belonged to a wealthy and highly visible sector of society, whether they were writing verse or erecting buildings, and their activities have left traces all out of proportion to their numbers."

19. Ibid., 51.

20. Ibid., 36.

21. Ibid., 43.

22. Ibid., 71–73.

23. Ibid., 70.

24. Ibid., 71.

25. Ibid., 72.

26. Ibid., 57. So too Harris, *Ancient Literacy*, 333.

27. Hezser, *Jewish Literacy*, 188.

28. On the various functions of literacy in ancient Rome, see Harris, *Ancient Literacy*, 196–218.

29. Ibid., 236.

30. Ibid., 237.

31. Ibid.

32. Ibid., 237–38.

33. Ibid., 238.

34. Hezser (*Jewish Literacy*, 170–76) similarly concludes that the rural and agricultural character of Roman Palestine would have resulted in little need for literate skills among the vast majority of the population.

35. My discussion on limited good, including the references to Foster's work below, is largely dependent on the fine essay of Jerome H. Neyrey and Richard L. Rohrbaugh, " 'He Must Increase, I Must Decrease' (John 3:30): A Cultural and Social Interpretation," in *The Social World of the New Testament: Insights and Models*, ed. Jerome H. Neyrey and Eric C. Stewart (Peabody, MA: Hendrickson, 2008), 237–51, here 237.

36. George M. Foster, "Peasant Society and the Image of Limited Good," *American Anthropologist* 67 (1965): 293–315, here 296.

37. George M. Foster, "The Anatomy of Envy: A Study in Symbolic Behavior," *Current Anthropology* 13 (1972): 165–202, here 169.

38. Neyrey and Rohrbaugh, "He Must Increase," 239.

39. See ibid., 240–49.

40. For a helpful and often cited discussion of the values of honor and shame, see Bruce J. Malina, *The New Testament World: Insights from Cultural Anthropology*, rev. ed. (Louisville, KY: Westminster John Knox, 2001), 27–57. The following summary of honor is indebted to Malina's discussion.

41. Ibid., 30.

42. Ibid., 33.

43. Ibid.

44. E.g., Malina (ibid., 36) states: "every social interaction that takes place outside of one's family or outside of one's circle of friends is perceived as a challenge to honor, a mutual attempt to acquire honor from one's social equal."

45. Morgan, *Literate Education*, 79.

46. Neyrey and Rohrbaugh, "He Must Increase," 239.

47. Morgan, *Literate Education*, 63.

48. Ibid., 65.

49. Hopkins, "Conquest by Book," 143.

50. Ibid., 144.

51. Ibid.

52. Ibid., 83.

53. Ibid., 74. See also 83, 103–4, 144–51, 226–39.

54. For a helpful discussion of the various social, economic and political functions of writing in the Roman world, see Harris, *Ancient Literacy*, 196–231.

55. Hopkins, "Conquest by Book," 137.

56. Ibid.

57. Ibid.

58. Mary Beard, "Writing and Religion: Ancient Literacy and the Function of the Written Word in Roman Religion," in *Literacy in the Roman World*, 35–60, here 39.

59. Ibid., 56–57. See also Richard Gordon, "From Republic to Principate: Priesthood, Religion and Ideology," in *Pagan Priests: Religion and Power in the Ancient World*, ed. M. Beard and J. North (Ithaca, NY: Cornell University Press, 1990), 179–98, esp. 184–91.

60. See Hezser, *Jewish Literacy*, 493–95.

Notes to Chapter 2 (pages 38–71)

1. For a detailed listing of the improvements Luke makes to Mark's style, see Joseph A. Fitzmyer, *The Gospel According to Luke I–IX*, Anchor Bible 28 (New York: Doubleday, 1981), 107–8.

2. Citing J. C. Hawkins, Fitzmyer (*Luke I–IX*, 109) states that of the words and phrases characteristic of the various Synoptic writers, ninety-five are distinctive of Matthew, forty-one of Mark, and 151 of Luke.

3. H. J. Cadbury, *The Style and Literary Method of Luke*, HTS 6 (Cambridge: Harvard University Press, 1920), 4–39.

4. Hans Conzelmann, *Acts of the Apostles*, trans. by James Limburg, et al., Hermeneia (Philadelphia: Fortress, 1987), xxxv.

5. François Bovon, *A Commentary on the Gospel of Luke 1:1–9:50*, trans. by Christine M. Thomas, Hermeia Commentary Series (Minneapolis: Fortress, 2002), 4.

6. Fitzmyer, *Luke I–IX*, 107.

7. Bovon, *Luke 1:1–9:50*, 17–18. David E. Aune (*The New Testament in Its Literary Environment*, Library of Early Christianity [Philadelphia: Westminster, 1987], 121) lists Josephus' *Against Apion* 1.1-5 and 2:1-2 (a two-volume work with primary and secondary prefaces) as among the closest of parallels to Luke's prefaces.

8. For a useful representation of the debate concerning Luke's prologue and the genres to which it points, see the essays in David P. Moessner, ed., *Jesus and the Heritage of Israel: Luke's Narrative Claim upon Israel's Legacy* (Harrisburg, PA: Trinity International Press, 1999).

9. For a concise summation of the debate regarding the genre of Luke, see Joel B. Green, *The Gospel of Luke*, NICNT (Grand Rapids, MI: Eerdmans, 1997), 2–6. For detailed treatments of the topic, see Aune, *Literary Environment*, 17–115, and Richard A. Burridge, *What Are the Gospels? A Comparison with Graeco-Roman Biography*, SNTSMS 70 (Cambridge: Cambridge University Press, 1992).

10. Adapted from Darrell L. Bock, *Luke 1:1–9:50*, BECNT (Grand Rapids: Baker, 1994), 51.

11. L. C. A. Alexander, "Luke's Preface in the Context of Greek Preface-Writing," *NovT* 28 (1986): 48–74.

12. Vernon K. Robbins, "The Claims of the Prologues and Greco-Roman Rhetoric: The Prefaces to Luke and Acts in Light of Greco-Roman Rhetorical Strategies," in *Jesus and the Heritage of Israel*, 66.

13. Fitzmyer, *Luke I–IX*, 109.

14. Charles H. Talbert, *Literary Patterns, Theological Themes and the Genre of Luke-Acts* (Atlanta: Scholars Press, 1974), 1.

15. This list of elements is an adaptation of that provided by Raymond Brown, *The Birth of the Messiah: A Commentary on the Infancy Narratives in the Gospels of Matthew and Luke*, rev. ed. (New York: Doubleday, 1993), 156. I have reproduced his listing in its entirety, with the exception of element 4, which Brown lists as "an objection by the visionary as to how this can be or a request for a sign." However, of the OT annunciations Brown lists as precedents (see p. 156: he reviews the annunciations of Ishmael [Gen 16:7-12], Isaac [Gen 17:1-8; 18:1-15], and Samson [Judg 13:1-23]), only the annunciations of Isaac's birth contains an objection and request for a sign. Such a request or objection is not present in Ishmael's annunciation, and what we find in Judges with the annunciation of Samson's birth (Judg 13:1-23) are neither requests for a sign nor an objection (as Brown indicates) but simply requests for more information (Judg 13:8, 17). Thus, instead of labeling this element as "an objection or request for a sign," I think it better to identify it more generally as "a response from the recipient."

16. Aune, *Literary Environment*, 122–23.

17. Ibid., 128.

18. Talbert, *Literary Patterns*, 67.

19. Ibid., 81.

20. For a more detailed articulation of this argument, please see Karl A. Kuhn, "The Point of the Step-Parallelism in Luke 1–2," *NTS* 47 (2001): 38–49.

21. Luke continues to imply that John prepares the way for Jesus throughout the following narrative. In the very next episode, in which the story lines of Jesus and John converge, the unborn John leaps upon the arrival of Mary (1:41) and in so doing appears to hail the advent of the recently conceived Jesus. Later, Zechariah proclaims the significance of his son in a canticle that is largely devoted to celebrating the arrival of God's promised salvation in the person of the Messiah (1:67-79). Finally, in 3:16, John answers those who were wondering if he was the Messiah, stating, "I baptize you with water; but one who is more powerful than I is coming; I am not worthy to untie the thong of his sandals. He will baptize you with the Holy Spirit and fire" (cf. Mark 1:7-8). Not only does this culminating episode again present Jesus as the one who is to come, it also continues Luke's emphasis on the exalted character of Jesus' person.

22. Stephen Usher, *The Historians of Greece and Rome* (London: Hamish Hamilton, 1969), 240.

23. Miller, "Dramatic Speech in the Roman Historians," *Greece & Rome* 22 (1975): 51.

24. Ibid., 51.

25. See Norma P. Miller, "Style and Content in Tacitus," in *Tacitus*, ed. T. A. Dorey (New York: Basic, 1969), 102–7; T. P. Wiseman, *Clio's Cosmetics: Three Studies in Greco-Roman Literature* (Rowman: Leicester University Press, 1979), 38; Michael Grant, *The Ancient Historians* (New York: Scribner, 1970), 292; Ronald Mellor, *Tacitus* (New York: Routledge, 1993), 114–16. See also Usher, *Historians of Greece and Rome*, 217.

26. F. W. Walbank, "Speeches in Greek Historians," The Third J. L. Myers Memorial Lecture (Oxford, 1965), 18. So also Walbank, *Polybius* (Berkeley: University of California Press, 1972), 45; Usher, *Historians of Greece and Rome*, 121–22. Offering a more critical appraisal of Polybius' reliability than most, Grant (*Ancient Historians*, 160) argues that Polybius' most elaborate speeches "are obviously fictitious from beginning to end." Grant adds that "what Polybius really wanted to achieve by such speeches [such as those of Hannibal and the consul Publius Scipio in Book 218] was to provide the sort of arguments which converted people from one cause to another. This seemed to him a good way of illustrating the dynamic interactions between one individual, or one group of individuals, and another."

27. Cited from Walbank's translation, *Polybius*, 12:25a-b.

28. Harold W. Attridge, "Ancient Historiography," in *Jewish Writings of the Second Temple Period*, ed. Michael E. Stone (Philadelphia: Fortress, 1984), 185–232.

29. John R. Bartlett, *The First and Second Book of Maccabees*, Cambridge Bible Commentaries on the Apocrypha (Cambridge: Cambridge University Press, 1973), 269.

30. Grant, *Ancient Historians*, 258.

31. Varneda, *The Historical Method of Flavius Josephus* (Leiden: E. J. Brill, 1986), 92–97.

32. H. St. John Thackeray, *Josephus—the Man and the Historian* (New York: Jewish Institute of Religion Press, 1929), 43.

33. Thackeray, *Josephus*, 43, 45.

34. B. Gärtner, *The Areopagus Speech and Natural Revelation*, ASNU 21 (Lund: C. W. K. Gleerup, 1955).

35. Gärtner, *Areopagus Speech*, 26.

36. For a historical survey of the study of the speeches of Acts, see the helpful overview provided by Marion Soards, *The Speeches in Acts: Their Content, Context, and Concerns* (Louisville: Westminster/John Knox, 1994), 1–11. See also the bibliography provided on the subject in Joel B. Green and Michael C. McKeever, *Luke-Acts and New Testament Historiography* (Grand Rapids, MI: Baker, 1994), 123–30.

37. Soards, *The Speeches in Acts*, 12. According to Soards (161), the distinctiveness of Luke's shaping of speeches is most evident in their "sheer repetitiveness," both in terms of the number of speeches and their content. This is also the case with the character speech in Luke 1–2 and 24. Even so, clear analogies to such repetition are found in both Greco-Roman and Israelite precedents as speeches were used to emphasize particular motifs. Luke, it appears, is further developing this already well-known use of character speech.

38. Ibid., 12.

39. Ibid.

40. Ibid., 183.

41. Karl Allen Kuhn, "In Their Own Words: Character Speech in the Gospel of Luke" (Ph.D. diss.; Marquette University, 1999).

42. Aune, *Literary Environment*, 83.

43. William S. Kurz, "Hellenistic Rhetoric in the Christological Proof of Luke-Acts," *CBQ* 42 (1980): 171–95, here 191.

44. Cited by Kenneth S. Sacks, "Rhetorical Approaches to Greek History Writing in the Hellenistic Period," SBLSP 23 (Missoula, MT: Scholars Press, 1984).

45. Kurz, "Hellenistic Rhetoric in Luke-Acts," 186.

46. Ibid., 176.

47. Ibid., 183.

48. See, e.g., Soards, *Speeches*; Ben Witherington III, *The Acts of the Apostles: A Socio-Rhetorical Commentary* (Grand Rapids, MI: Eerdmans, 1998); Joseph A. Fitzmyer, *The Acts of the Apostles*, Anchor Bible 31 (New York: Doubleday, 1998); Luke Timothy Johnson, *The Acts of the Apostles*, Sacra Pagina 5 (Collegeville, MN: Liturgical Press, 1992); Hans Conzelmann, *Acts of the*

Apostles, trans. by James Lindberg, et al. Hermeneia (Philadelphia: Fortress, 1987).

49. P. E. Satterthwaite, "Acts against the Background of Classical Rhetoric," in *The Book of Acts in Its Ancient Literary Setting*, ed. Bruce Winter and Andrew D. Clarke, vol. 1 (Grand Rapids, MI: Eerdmans, 1993), 337–80, here 378.

50. Ibid., 379.

51. For a helpful discussion of ancient rhetorical theory and the role of pathos as a primary means of persuasion, see Thomas H. Olbricht, "*Pathos* as Proof in Greco-Roman Rhetoric," in *Paul and Pathos*, ed. Thomas H. Olbricht and Jerry L. Sumney, SBL Symposium Series 16 (Atlanta: Society of Biblical Literature, 2001), 8–22. See also Mario M. DiCicco, *Paul's Use of Ethos, Pathos and Logos in 2 Corinthians 10–13*, Mellen Biblical Press Series 31 (Lewiston, NY: Mellen, 1995), 16–28.

52. See Olbricht and Sumney, *Paul and Pathos*, 39–202; DiCicco, *Paul's Use*. Steven J. Kraftchick ("Pathē in Paul: The Emotional Logic of 'Original Argument,'" in *Paul and Pathos*, 53–55) points out that in the writings of the later Roman rhetoricians of Cicero and Quintilian, *ethos* and *pathos* came to be regarded as degrees of emotional response that could sway the objections of a jury or audience. *Ethos* came to refer to milder forms of emotional appeal, including but not limited to the character of the speaker, and *pathos* to fervent emotions.

53. Aristotle, *Poetics*, 4.1. This translation from Aristotle, *Poetics*, trans. Malcom Heath (New York: Penguin, 1996). The precise meaning of *katharsis* here is hotly debated among scholars, and Heath ("Introduction," *Poetics*, lxix, n. 15) reports that no consensus on the term has emerged. I used the ambiguous "more complete understanding" above to capture the lowest common denominator of what most scholars addressing the issue would affirm.

54. Quintilian, *Institutes*, 4.2.111, cited in James W. Thompson, "Paul's Argument from *Pathos* in 2 Corinthians," in *Paul and Pathos*, 127.

55. Quintilian, *Institutes*, 6.2.26, cited in DiCicco, *Paul's Use*, 129.

56. DiCicco, *Paul's Use*, 130, citing Quintilian, *Institutes*, 6.2.29-32.

57. Karl Allen Kuhn, *The Heart of Biblical Narrative: Rediscovering Biblical Appeal to the Emotions* (Minneapolis: Fortress, 2009).

58. Green, *Luke*, 67.

59. As Green (ibid., 65) notes: "Given the preceding affirmations, v. 7 is startling."

60. Brown (*Birth*, 279) argues that in having Zechariah object Luke is following an established annunciation form carrying over from the OT traditions, which includes an objection or request for a sign. Recall, however, my earlier adaptation of Brown's listing of the annunciation form, where

I argued that such objections are not as common as simple requests for more information. Thus, instead of labeling this element as "an objection or request for a sign," it would be better to indentify it more generally as "a response from the recipient."

61. Green, *Luke*, 79.

62. As pronounced by Reginald H. Fuller (*The Formation of the Resurrection Narratives* [New York: Macmillan, 1971], 104): "It is universally agreed that the Emmaus story is a gem of literary art."

Notes to Chapter 3 (pages 72–101)

1. Based on his own investigation of Luke's social location, Vernon K. Robbins ("The Social Location of the Implied Author of Luke-Acts," in *The Social World of Luke-Acts: Models for Interpretation*, ed. Jerome H. Neyrey ([Peabody, MA: Hendrickson, 1991], 320) argues that "the thought of the implied author is located near the artisan class." The evidence leading him to this assessment is Luke's apparent familiarity with artisan technology and the "dynamics of life at this level of society," as displayed by his depiction of artisans and their craft primarily in Acts (e.g., 16:14; 18:1-3; 19:23-24; 27:1-20). In my view, these brief references to artisan technology simply do not bear the weight Robbins places upon them as potential indicators of Luke's own social location but reflect knowledge available to anyone who would have had the experience of living in a city or traveling by sea. At the same time, Robbins notes Luke's familiarity with grammar and rhetoric (319) and also suggests that Luke had the intent of writing his work for the elite, as indicated by the work's address to the "most excellent Theophilus" (320–23). Whether for Robbins Luke was actually of the "artisan class" or simply identified with them in some fashion, Robbins doesn't say, nor does he explore the implications of Luke's literary artistry for understanding his social location.

2. This brief review is dependent on Richard S. Ascough's summary of social rank in *Lydia: Paul's Cosmopolitan Hostess*, Paul's Social Network Series (Collegeville, MN: Liturgical Press, 2009), 59–60.

3. Richard Rohrbaugh, "The Social Location of the Markan Audience," in *The Social World of the New Testament: Insights and Models*, ed. Jerome H. Neyrey and Eric C. Stewart (Peabody, MA: Hendrickson, 2008), 148.

4. Rohrbaugh, "Social Location," 145–46.

5. K. C. Hanson and Douglas E. Oakman, *Palestine in the Time of Jesus: Social Structures and Social Conflicts*, 2nd ed. (Minneapolis: Fortress, 2008), 65.

6. Ibid., 66.

7. Rohrbaugh, "Social Location," 154. The two studies cited by Rohrbaugh are Joseph Zias, "Death and Disease in Ancient Israel," *Biblical Archaeologist* 54 (1991): 146–59; and David A. Fiensy, *The Social History of Palestine in the Herodian Period: The Land is Mine*, Studies in the Bible and Early Christianity 20 (Lewiston, NY: Mellen, 1991).

8. Rohrbaugh, "Social Location," 150, 151.

9. "Fictive" or "pseudo" kinship groups refer to groups of clients constituted by their commitment to a common patron and are governed by the roles, obligations, and responsibilities between the patron and his or her clients and by the clients' mutual calling to remain loyal to the patron and to some extent one another.

10. Bruce J. Malina, *The New Testament World: Insights from Cultural Anthropology*, 3rd ed. (Louisville, KY: Westminster John Knox, 2001), 83.

11. E.g., B. S. Easton, "The Purpose of Luke-Acts," in *Early Christianity: The Purpose of Acts, and Other Papers*, ed. F. C. Grant (Greenwich, CT: Seabury, 1954), 31–118; Ernst Haenchen, *The Acts of the Apostles: A Commentary* (Philadelphia: Fortress, 1971); Philip Esler, *Community and Gospel in Luke-Acts: The Social and Political Motivations of Lucan Theology*, SNTSMS 57 (Cambridge: Cambridge University Press, 1987); Gregory E. Sterling, *Historiography and Self-Definition: Josephos, Luke-Acts, and Apologetic Historiography*, NovTSup 64 (Leiden: Brill, 1992); Brigitte Kahl, "Acts of the Apostles: Pro(to)-Imperial Script and Hidden Transcript," in *In the Shadow of Empire*, ed. Richard A. Horsley (Louisville, KY: Westminster John Knox, 2008), 137–56.

12. Ben Witherington III, *New Testament History: A Narrative Account* (Grand Rapids, MI: Baker Academic, 2001), 383.

13. For helpful reviews of various theories regarding the purpose of Luke-Acts, see Darrell L. Bock, *Luke 1:1–9:50*, ECNT (Grand Rapids, MI: Baker, 1994), 14–15; Mark Allan Powell, *What Are They Saying about Acts?* (New York: Paulist, 1991), 13–19; Joseph A. Fitzmyer, *The Gospel According to Luke I–IX*, AB 28 (New York: Doubleday, 1981), 8–13.

14. See, e.g., Richard Horsley, *The Liberation of Christmas: The Infancy Narratives in Social Context* (New York: Crossroad, 1989); Halvor Moxnes, "Patron-Client Relations and the New Community in Luke-Acts," in *The Social World of Luke-Acts*, 241–70; Joel B. Green, *The Gospel of Luke*, NICNT (Grand Rapids, MI: Eerdmans, 1997), 9, 23–25; Karl Allen Kuhn, *The Heart of Biblical Narrative* (Minneapolis: Fortress, 2008), 63–138.

15. It is true that the proud, rich, and powerful do symbolize for Luke those who have strayed from God and embraced another Lord. But this is not because the *economic* realities such figures represent are insignificant for Luke. On the contrary, it is their participation in an economy that deprives many of the necessities of life that marks them as those who counter God's designs for creation.

16. I am dependent here on John H. Elliot's fine essay, "Temple versus Household in Luke-Acts: A Contrast in Social Institutions," in *The Social World of Luke-Acts*, 211–40.

17. Ibid., 236.

18. Ibid. See also Moxnes, "Patron-Client Relations," 266.

19. Green, *Luke*, 122. For a helpful discussion of how the census would be perceived by most Israelites as a particularly egregious instance of oppressive Roman hegemony, see Horsley, *The Liberation of Christmas*, 33–38.

20. Helpful overviews of the debate can be found in Fitzmyer, *Luke I–IX*, 400–405; John Nolland, *Luke 1:1–9:20*, WBC 35a (Waco, TX: Word, 1989), 99–103; and Bock, *Luke 1:1–9:50*, 903–9.

21. As similarly noted by Brown, *Birth*, 415; Fitzmyer, *Luke I–IX*, 393; Green, *Luke*, 121–22;

22. Bock's (*Luke 1:1–9:50*, 208) description of Joseph and Mary's lodgings is representative of most recent commentators:

> The mention of the feed trough does suggest that Jesus was born in an animal room of some sort. But what kind of animal room was it and why were the child's parents there? The passage tells us that they were there because (*dioti*) there was no room for them at the *katalumati* (*katalumati*, public shelter). *Kataluma* suggests that a formal inn is not in view here. . . . Rather, *kataluma* seems to refer to some type of reception room in a private home or some type of public shelter. Since this place was full, refuge was sought elsewhere.

23. Green, *Luke*, 130–31.

24. The reversal in play here may be directed not only at Rome but also at Jerusalem and the temple. Green (*Luke*, 131) states:

> Given the respect assigned earlier to the Jerusalem temple and particularly to its sanctuary as the *axis mundi*—the meeting place between the heavenly and the earthly, the divine and human—this appearance of the divine glory is remarkable. God's glory, normally associated with the temple, is now manifest on a farm! At the birth of his son, God has compromised (in a proleptic way) the socio-religious importance of the temple as the cultural center of the world of Israel. Luke thus puts us on notice that the new world coming is of a radically different shape than the former one, that questions of holiness and purity must be asked and addressed in different ways, and that status and issues of values must be reexamined afresh.

25. Translation from S. R. F. Price, *Rituals and Power: The Roman Imperial Cult in Asia Minor* (Cambridge: Cambridge University Press, 1984), 54; emphasis added.

26. Horsley, *Liberation of Christmas*, 32–33.

27. Josephus, *Wars*, 6.312-13, cited in Adam Winn, *The Purpose of Mark's Gospel: An Early Christian Response to Roman Imperial Propaganda*, WUNT 245 (Tübingen: Mohr Siebeck, 2008), 161.

28. Tacitus, *History*, 5.13.1-2, cited in Winn, *Mark's Gospel*, 161.

29. Scholars are divided over whether the references *panti tō laō* ("all the people") and *en anthrōpois eudokias* ("among those whom God favors") should be understood as referring only to faithful Israelites or if they are inclusive of Gentiles as well. Most commentators take the expressions "all the people" and "among those whom God favors" as references only to Israel. It is typically pointed out that Luke often utilizes the phrase "all the people" without any emphasis on *pas* in a universalistic sense and that with the exception of Acts 15:14 and 18:10 the normal use of the singular *laos* refers to Israel (Luke 3:21; 7:29; 8:47; 18:43; 19:48; 21:38; 24:19; Acts 4:10; 13:24). Stephen G. Wilson (*The Gentiles and the Gentile Mission in Luke-Acts*, SNTSMS 23 [Cambridge: Cambridge University Press, 1973], 34–35) infers from this evidence that: "Thus, while admitting that a reference to the new people of God, both Israelites and Gentiles, is possible in 2:10, we conclude that it is unlikely." Wilson is followed in his judgment by the majority of commentators, including Raymond Brown (*The Birth of the Messiah: A Commentary on the Infancy Narratives in Matthew and Luke*, rev ed. [New York: Doubleday, 1993], 402); I. Howard Marshall (*The Gospel of Luke: A Commentary on the Greek Text*, NIGTC 3 [Grand Rapids, MI: Eerdmans, 1978], 109); Mark Coleridge (*The Birth of the Lukan Narrative: Narrative and Christology in Luke 1–2*, JSNTSup 88 [Sheffield: JSOT, 1993], 139 n. 2); Nolland (*Luke 1:1–9:20*, 107); and Bock (*Luke 1:1–9:50*, 215); contra Green, *Luke*, 134, n. 54.

Yet, it should also be pointed out that in each of the occurrences of the phrase throughout Luke-Acts it is the *context* that establishes who is in view. For Luke, there is nothing intrinsic to the phrase itself that indicates that it is to refer exclusively to Israel, as evidenced by its use to indicate both Israelites and Gentiles in Acts 15:14 and 18:10 and by the use of the qualifier "of Israel" in Acts 4:10 and 13:24 where the context would otherwise not indicate to whom the expression refers. Moreover, there are several reasons for perceiving that in this passage Luke introduces what he will much more directly relay in the following episode (2:32): the salvific significance of God's act of salvation in Jesus for both Israel *and* Gentiles. First, as discussed above, Luke's casting of this episode against a background of world history has already implied a universal significance for Jesus' birth. Second, the couplet parallelism of v. 14 places the realm of *en hupsitois* ("in the highest") in apposition to *epi gēs* ("upon the earth"), with the implication that Jesus' birth is proclaimed as an event that impacts both heavenly and earthly reality. This expansive, spatial imagery suggests that the peace accomplished in Jesus' advent is cosmic in scope. Third, the presentation of Jesus as the true Lord and Savior in contrast to Caesar clearly implies that Jesus' sovereignty *and* salvific rule extend beyond the borders of his relatively small homeland and similarly encompass "all the world."

Note to Conclusion (pages 102–106)

1. For a well-articulated argument that Luke was an Israelite priest, see Rick Strelan, *Luke the Priest: The Authority of the Author of the Third Gospel* (Burlington: Ashgate, 2008).

BIBLIOGRAPHY

Alexander, L. C. A. "Luke's Preface in the Context of Greek Preface-Writing." *NovT* 28 (1986): 48–74.

Aristotle. *Poetics*. Malcom Heath, trans. New York: Penguin, 1996.

Attridge, Harold W. "Ancient Historiography," in *Jewish Writings of the Second Temple Period*, 185–232. Michael E. Stone, ed. Philadelphia: Fortress, 1984.

Aune, David E. *The New Testament in Its Literary Environment*. Library of Early Christianity. Philadelphia: Westminster, 1987.

Barrett, Charles K. "Paul Shipwrecked," in *Scripture, Meaning and Method*, 51–63. B. P. Thompson, ed. Hull: Hull University Press, 1987.

Bartlett, John R. *The First and Second Book of Maccabees*. Cambridge Bible Commentaries on the Apocrypha. Cambridge: Cambridge University Press, 1973.

Beard, Mary. "Writing and Religion: Ancient Literacy and the Function of the Written Word in Roman Religion," in *Literacy in the Roman World*, 35–60. J. H. Humphrey, ed. Journal of Roman Archaeology Supplementary Series 3. Ann Arbor: University of Michigan, 1991.

Bock, Darrell L. *Luke 1:1–9:50*. BECNT. Grand Rapids: Baker, 1994.

Bovon, François. *A Commentary on the Gospel of Luke 1:1–9:50*. Trans. by Christine M. Thomas. Hermeia Commentary Series. Minneapolis: Fortress, 2002.

Brawley, Robert. *Luke-Acts and Jews: Conflict, Apology and Conciliation*. Atlanta: Scholars Press, 1987.

Brooke, George. "Luke-Acts and the Qumran Scrolls: The Case of the MMT," in *Luke's Literary Achievement*, 72–90. *JSNTSup* 116. Sheffield: Sheffield Academic Press, 1995.

Brown, Raymond. *The Birth of the Messiah: A Commentary on the Infancy Narratives in the Gospels of Matthew and Luke*. Rev. ed. New York: Doubleday, 1993.

Burridge, Richard A. *What are the Gospels? A Comparison with Graeco-Roman Biography*. SNTSMS 70. Cambridge: Cambridge University Press, 1992.

Cadbury, H. J. *The Style and Literary Method of Luke*. HTS 6. Cambridge: Harvard University Press, 1920.

Conzelmann, Hans. *Acts of the Apostles*. Trans. by James Limburg et al. Hermeneia. Philadelphia: Fortress, 1987.

Crenshaw, James L. *Education in Ancient Israel: Across the Deadening Silence*. New York: Doubleday, 1998.

DiCicco, Mario M. *Paul's Use of Ethos, Pathos and Logos in 2 Corinthians 10–13*. Mellen Biblical Press Series 31. Lewiston, NY: Mellen, 1995.

Elliot, John H. "Jesus the Israelite was Neither a Jew or a Christian." *JSHJ* 5 (2007): 119–54.

Fitzmyer, Joseph A. *The Gospel According to Luke I–IX*. AB 28. New York: Doubleday, 1981.

———. *Luke the Theologian: Aspects of His Teaching*. Mahwah: Paulist, 1989.

———. *The Acts of the Apostles*. AB 31. New York: Doubleday, 1997.

Foster, George M. "Peasant Society and the Image of Limited Good." *American Anthropologist* 67 (1965): 293–315.

———. "The Anatomy of Envy: A Study in Symbolic Behavior." *Current Anthropology* 13 (1972): 165–202.

Gärtner, B. *The Areopagus Speech and Natural Revelation*. ASNU 21. Lund: C. W. K. Gleerup, 1955.

Gordon, Richard. "From Republic to Principate: Priesthood, Religion and Ideology, " in *Pagan Priests: Religion and Power in the Ancient World*, 179–98. M. Beard and J. North, eds. Ithaca: Cornell University Press, 1990.

Grant, Michael, *The Ancient Historians*. New York: Scribners, 1970.

Green, Joel B. *The Gospel of Luke*. NICNT. Grand Rapids: Eerdmans, 1997.

———, and Michael C. McKeever. *Luke-Acts and New Testament Historiography*. Grand Rapids: Baker, 1994.

Haenchen, Ernst. " 'We' in Acts and the Itinerary," in *The Bultmann School of Biblical Interpretation: New Directions?*, 590–68. JTC 1. Tübingen: Mohr. New York: Harper, 1965.

Harris, William V. *Ancient Literacy*. Cambridge, MA: Harvard University Press, 1989.

Hezser, Catherine. *Jewish Literacy in Roman Palestine*. Texts and Studies in Ancient Palestine, 81. Tübingen: Mohr-Siebeck, 2001.

Horsley, Richard. *The Liberation of Christmas: The Infancy Narrative in Social Context*. New York: Crossroad, 1989.

Humphrey, J. H., ed. *Literacy in the Roman World*. Journal of Roman Archaeology Supplementary Series 3. Ann Arbor: University of Michigan, 1991.

Jafee, Martin. *Torah in the Mouth: Writing and Oral Tradition in Palestinian Judaism, 200 BCE–400 CE*. New York: Oxford University Press, 2001.

Johnson, Luke Timothy. *The Acts of the Apostles*. Sacra Pagina 5. Collegeville, MN: Liturgical Press, 1992.

Kuhn, Karl A. "The Point of the Step-Parallelism in Luke 1–2." *NTS* 47 (2001): 38–49.

———. "The 'One like a Son of Man' Becomes the 'Son of God.'" *CBQ* 69 (2007): 22–42.

———. *The Heart of Biblical Narrative: Rediscovering Biblical Appeal to the Emotions*. Minneapolis: Fortress, 2009.

Kurz, William S. "Hellenistic Rhetoric in the Christological Proof of Luke-Acts." *CBQ* 42 (1980): 171–95.

Malina, Bruce J. *The New Testament World: Insights from Cultural Anthropology*. Rev. ed. Louisville: Westminster John Knox, 2001.

Mellor, Richard. *Tacitus*. New York: Routledge, 1993.

Miller, Norma P. "Style and Content in Tacitus," in *Tacitus*, 102–107. T. A. Dorey, ed. New York: Basic, 1969.

———. "Dramatic Speech in the Roman Historians," *Greece & Rome* 22 (1975): 45–56.

Moessner, David P., ed. *Jesus and the Heritage of Israel: Luke's Narrative Claim upon Israel's Legacy*. Harrisburg, PA: Trinity International Press, 1999.

Morgan, Teresa. *Literate Education in the Hellenistic and Roman Worlds*. Cambridge Classical Studies. Cambridge: Cambridge University Press, 1998.

Neyrey, Jerome H., and Richard L. Rohrbaugh, "'He Must Increase, I Must Decrease' (John 3:30): A Cultural and Social Interpretation," in *The Social World of the New Testament: Insights and Models*, 237–51. Jerome H. Neyrey and Eric C. Stewart, eds. Peabody, MA: Hendrickson, 2008.

Olbricht, Thomas H. "*Pathos* as Proof in Greco-Roman Rhetoric," in *Paul and Pathos*, 8–22. Thomas H. Olbricht and Jerry L. Sumney, eds. SBL Symposium Series 16. Atlanta: Society of Biblical Literature, 2001.

Robbins, Vernon K. "By Land and by Sea: The We Passages and Ancient Sea Voyages," in *Perspectives in Luke-Acts*, 215–42. C. H. Talbert, ed. Edinburg: T & T Clark, 1978.

Sattherthwaite, P. E. "Acts Against the Background of Classical Rhetoric," in *The Book of Acts in its Ancient Literary Setting*, 337–80. Bruce Winter and Andrew D. Clarke, eds. vol 1. Grand Rapids: Eerdmans, 1993.

Snyder, H. Gregory. *Teachers and Texts in the Ancient World: Philosophers, Israelites and Christians*. Religion in the First Christian Centuries. New York: Routledge, 2000.

Soards, Marion. *The Speeches in Acts: Their Content, Context and Concerns*. Louisville: Westminster/John Knox, 1994.

Strelan, Rick. *Luke, the Priest: The Authority of the Author of the Third Gospel*. Burlington: Ashgate, 2008.

Talbert, Charles H. *Literary Patterns, Theological Themes and the Genre of Luke-Acts*. Atlanta: Scholars Press, 1974.

Thackeray, H. St. John. *Josephus—the Man and the Historian*. New York: Jewish Institute of Religion Press, 1929.

Usher, Stephen. *The Historians of Greece and Rome*. London: Hamish Hamilton, 1969.

Varneda, Pere. *The Historical Method of Flavius Josephus*. Leiden: E. J. Brill, 1986.

Walbank, F. W. *Polybius*. Berkeley: University of California Press, 1972.

Wehnert, Jürgen. *Die Wir-Passagagen der Apostelgeschichte: Ein lukanisches Stilmittel aus jüdischer Tradition*. Göttingen: Vandenhoeck & Ruprecht, 1989.

———. "The Claims of the Prologues and Greco-Roman Rhetoric: The Prefaces to Luke and Acts in Light of Greco-Roman Rhetorical Strategies," in *Jesus and the Heritage of Israel: Luke's Narrative Claim upon Israel's Legacy*, 63–83. David P. Moessner, ed. Harrisburg, PA: Trinity International Press, 1999.

Wiseman, T. P. *Clio's Cosmetics: Three Studies in Greco-Roman Literature*. Rowman: Leicester University Press, 1979.

Witherington III, Ben. *Acts of the Apostles: A Social-Rhetorical Commentary*. Grand Rapids: Eerdmans, 1998.

INDEX OF PERSONS AND SUBJECTS

SCRIPTURE AND
ANCIENT WRITERS INDEX